How to Avoid Huge Ships

HOW TO AVOID HUGE SHIPS

or
I Never Met a Ship I Liked

by
Captain John W. Trimmer

Published by Captain John W. Trimmer,
2932 25th West, Seattle, Washington 98199.
Printed in the United States of America
by The National Writers Press, Aurora, Colorado.

International Standard Book Number: 0-88100-019-1

Library of Congress Number: 82-061398

To my wife Jewel,
my second pilot and anchor to windward
whenever the ship started to run off course
with a broken rudder and a busted engine.

Table of Contents

ABOUT THE AUTHOR

Captain John W. Trimmer was fifteen years old when he first stepped aboard a tug boat on Seattle's waterfront to begin what is still today an active thirty-nine year maritime career. He has served aboard almost every type of vessel ranging in size from giant troop ships carrying thousands of men, and fast freighters carrying millions of dollars of cargo, to captain of sturdy ocean-going tug boats bound for Alaska and the Asian countries of the Far East.

After thirty-two years at sea, fifty-five year old Captain Trimmer took on a second career, this time as a ship's pilot. He started in the Panama Canal, then five years ago began working as a pilot on the waters of Puget Sound in the state of Washington.

Out of his vast experiences he has written this book for the captain/owners of small boats. This book contains information that should have been given to private boat captains years ago.

The photo above shows John Trimmer (left) standing on the bridge wing aboard a large modern container ship before leaving the dock. He and the ship's Captain are discussing the up-coming sixty-nine mile trip from Seattle to the Port Angeles Pilot Station where the Master will take over for the trans-Pacific run to the Far East.

FOREWORD

If over the years I had been given a dollar each time a small boat has sailed into near danger and looming disaster by steering close under the flaring bow of a ship where I was serving as pilot, I would be a wealthy man today. But alas no one has ever given me a dollar, and most likely never will.

The writing of this book was prompted by the many near misses, impending collisions and close calls involving thousands of pleasure craft that happened during the years I worked as captain and mate aboard large tugs towing huge barges, not to mention the almost collisions that took place while serving as a pilot on the bridge of ships both in the United States and the Panama Canal.

This book is not intended as a criticism of any kind directed to the captains and operators of smaller vessels. Instead it is my fervent hope and desire that *How to Avoid Huge Ships or I never Met a Ship I Liked* will serve as a guide and best friend to the captain of a private vessel when he finds himself in a tight situation with a large ship, whether the commander be an occasional weekend sailor or a steady year around navigator.

These days while I stand on the bridge of a heavily loaded ship with binoculars in hand, surrounded by dials, levers, lights and the latest navigational aids including two well tuned radars, I continually marvel at the captain who can with skill and daring, maneuver a swift moving sailing vessel in a stiff wind, keeping the boat safe as it cuts through the water under a huge spread of canvas. I envy the expert maneuvering done by the commander of a power craft whose white hull remains unscratched due to practised handling, while I am constrained with a big ship whose high, stiff sides and wide bows make it a cumbersome, unwieldy giant waiting for an accident to happen. I am constantly aware the ships I pilot are slow to turn, difficult to stop, and consistently maneuver like a sick cow. In some instances it seems they cannot even get out of their own way, and unfortunately their speed through the water while underway gives the distant observer, and more particularly the nearby commander of a smaller vessel, just the opposite impression. **This miscalculation can quickly lure the unwary into great danger!**

This book is not intended to replace the official "Rules of the Road." It is written with one purpose: to give you a simple and practical guide to keep you out from under the massive bows of commercial vessels. In all cases these are bigger and often faster than yours.

Over the years I have looked in vain for a book I could buy and give to my boating friends: a book they could carry with them and use at the scene as they forged into the shipping lanes of the nation's harbors, bays and waterways, a busy place where the ships hurriedly plow their way back and forth to the ocean from whence they came. I hope this publication will give the captain of a smaller vessel some degree of assurance that what he is doing around these deep draft vessels will prevent his craft from ever coming close to being run down by some over-size ship. **I pray it will keep you and yours *out of harm's way!***

PROLOGUE

Consider this: a person cannot legally drive an automobile without first possessing a driver's license. But he can drive a boat without a single piece of paper in hand saying he is qualified to do so. Yet of the two, the boat by far requires more training and skill to operate safely than any automobile ever placed on the road. The same person who wouldn't dream of driving a truck without prior instruction, practice and examination, will spend thousands of dollars for a boat and yet never learn how to properly and safely keep it out of the way of other vessels, whether they be big or small. I am sure each of us can tell more than one story about a person who has spent large sums of money for a fine boat. Then he listened very carefully to a long list of instructions on how to start the engine, turn on the lights, tune in the AM/FM radio, pump the bilges, etc., after which he takes off from the dock without the most rudimentary knowledge in his head concerning the Rules of the Road, and how to avoid a collision. Hopefully someone will be around just before he leaves the dock to hand him or her a copy of this little book so even if he doesn't know the rules, at least he will recognize the dangers he faces and thereby save his life and that of other poor souls aboard his hazardous moving craft.

I said earlier that this was not a book about Rules of the Road, and it is not. However, I can't avoid touching on the subject briefly.

It is an unfortunate fact of life for many of us, that those things in life which are hard to learn and difficult to do, will only be accomplished with great effort. This is no more apparent than in an attempt to learn, understand and properly apply the Rules of the Road. Even for the professional master, mate or pilot, the subject of the rules are difficult to retain in memory and apply correctly and consistently. This then leaves every commander uncertain at times of just when or how to decide the rules in an extreme situation. A wrong decision made in the heat of the moment at sea can be found at fault in court at a later date.

It is indeed unfortunate that collisions have occurred and will continue to happen because the rules were disregarded by one or more vessels in a meeting or crossing situation.

If the professional seaman on the bridge of a ship is incapable of consistently applying the correct rule in a given situation, either through ignorance, a faulty memory, or lack of a clear understanding of what specific rule applies in a given circumstance, how, then, is the part time sailor to avoid getting into a close situation when his vessel is in immediate danger of being run over? You can study the rules until your eyes fall out of your head, but if you cannot recall the one rule that fits your particular situation just before some large ship is about to hit you broadside, then a study of the rules has failed you just at the time you needed them most. *This book is, I hope, the answer when doubt sets in,* **as your craft and some approaching ship are headed toward the exact same spot on the crowded sea lanes!**

Consider if you will for a moment the following article appearing in the newspaper *Seattle Post Intelligencer* on June 2, 1982:

FOG AND FRIGHT IN THE STRAITS
RECALLED BY RACE PARTICIPANTS

"It was terrifying."

Those words of a Swiftsure skipper were repeated time and again with slight variations by sailors who came in out of the fog from the Northwest's top yachting event over the past weekend.

It's hardly surprising, considering the ingredients and the circumstances.

Take more than 450 sailboats of various sizes with a wide range of navigational equipment, mix in an assortment of ocean-going commercial vessels with a distressing lack of control, then garnish with a heavy layer of fog.

Under those conditions, it's amazing there haven't been more reports of boats banging into each other or sailors getting run down and sunk by a huge freighter. Stories of what were near misses could have ended in disaster.

While many of the lead boats in this year's Swiftsure and Juan de Fuca races up the Strait and back to Victoria managed to avoid the fog, others were not so fortunate.

Crew members aboard Wind Child, Marda Runstad's Ranger 28, estimated they came within roughly 10 seconds of being cut in half by a commercial ship in the wee small hours of the morning Sunday. Visibility was almost zero in the heavy fog as the boat was moving well, spinnaker flying.

"The ship looked about the size of a hotel, coming right at us," Runstad said later. "I've never been so terrified in all my years of sailing."

Barely slipping past the freighter, the sailboat almost turned turtle from the wake of the ship, which showed no sign of slowing down as it churned up the Strait. The shaken but happy-to-be-alive crew on Wind Child took down the Spinnaker and headed for the Canadian shore, only to come within a whisker of hitting a huge rock not far from the entrance to Sooke Harbor.

—Reproduced with permission of the *Seattle Post Intelligencer*, copyright 1982.

Chapter One

What You Should Know Ships and Engines

The pounding engine sitting in the bottom of the average ship as it hurries past, plowing up the ocean, is probably diesel powered. This type of engine is easily recognized by the throbbing and rumbling sound it creates in passing, as the heavy black oil is sucked out of the tanks and shot into the rapidly firing pistons. Nine out of every ten ships I climb aboard at the pilot station are motor ships. This being true, it is best you know and understand the workings and limitations of a large diesel engine. The first and most important thing you should know is they cannot be thrown into reverse quickly while running full ahead. This is one of several limitations concerning the maneuvering characteristics of ships powered with diesel engines.

Knowledge about the shortcomings of a motor ship's power plant may some day save your life, if only because after reading this book you will understand the limitations imposed on a pilot when ordering speed changes to a machine producing thousands of horse power. It is a machine built so large in size it dwarfs any other single moving power plant in the world. Once set in motion, it is a fire breathing monster running almost out of control. They have been known to run away with their own momentum and blow apart, or experience an explosion that will set an entire engine room to burning. These fires and explosions often leave dead engineers scattered over the engine room floor plates. The size of this huge, almost living creature makes it possible to move large, deep draft ships through the water at a high speed and, hopefully, for the owner, at a cheap cost.

1

Lest you believe I am exaggerating the problems of a marine diesel engine blowing up in what is called a base explosion, allow me to tell you a true but frightening happening I experienced some years ago. I was chief mate aboard a large ocean-going tug sailing out of Seattle. One night enroute to Sitka, Alaska, the tug was pulling a huge barge loaded with twenty rail tank cars filled with chlorine gas and liquid sulphur. In the hold of the barge twelve hundred tons of caustic acid sloshed around in the cargo tanks. The entire barge was a potent and dangerous mess.

We had been underway about an hour when the chief engineer watching the engine temperatures rise to proper level, increased the speed to full ahead and left the engine room. The barge, wide as a World War II Liberty ship, was on a towline eight hundred feet long and was tracking directly astern at seven and one half knots.

Aboard the tug my small but tidy room was located on the main deck, starboardside forward. It was directly over the starboardside of the engine room. My room had two doors. One door led to the room aft, and this room was fitted with a door leading to the outside. My room had no door to the outside. The second door of my room opened directly into the engine room fiddley (the portion of the engine room space above the engine, or the upper half of the engine room if you will). Through this fiddley I was able to pass to the interior spaces of the tug.

That night, standing in my room within arm's length of the door opening to the fiddley, I could hear the engine going to full power after warm up. Shortly a terrible explosion took place. Instantly the door in my room leading to the fiddley exploded inward. Sheets of flame came blasting through the open door, mixed with volumes of heavy, oily smoke. Luckily I was able to reach over and slam the door shut. Fire and smoke filled the engine room and fiddley where the flames roared like the fires of hell. The flames came so quickly into my room the hair on my head was burned and my eyelashes badly singed. Through the room aft I escaped to the outside deck. Fortunately just before the explosion the chief engineer had left the engine room on an errand.

After checking to make sure the crew had all gathered outside safe on deck, the chief and I made for the wheelhouse. There we activated the discharge valves connecting to a bank of CO-2 cylinders in the engine room. The fire was extinguished in a matter of minutes. Unfortunately the tug was left drifting, smoldering, a useless wreck.

In the wheelhouse, three decks above the engine room, the force of the explosion knocked the captain off his feet. The wheelhouse was filled with thick smoke and drifting soot. The explosion knocked out the steering gear. The tug with a destroyed engine was unable to maneuver. Due to loss of power the tug lugged down like an old log and began to drift backwards pulled by the weight of the underwater deep-sea towing gear weighing many tons. The tug lay helpless in the path of the barge still making a speed of seven and one half knots.

Shortly the barge was upon the tug and struck the helpless vessel in the stern. The barge was constructed with a shovel nose type bow (similar to the bow of a Coast Guard ice breaker), and rode up on top of the tug's stern. This forced the tug's stern down into the water until the cold sea water was running over the after deck in a strong flood. Then the natural buoyancy of the tug came into play and forced the tug out from under the barge. The tug, now beginning to twist, shot out from under the weight of the barge like a cork popping out of a bottle. The force of buoyancy shoved the tug ahead of the moving barge. The tug after twisting sharply to starboard went dead in the water a second time. The barge hit the tug a glancing blow, this time square amidship.

The crew was alert and active in spite of the heavy smoke all around and managed to lasso the barge with a deck line as the barge moved past at a lively speed. It required two months in the shipyard to put the tug back together.

Warning: Give tugs and ships a wide berth, as my shipmates and I learned. Diesel vessels can quickly get out of control, thus leaving the crew helpless to take evasive action to avoid running down any unwary vessels nearby!

1—Engine Failures — for years I sailed aboard tugboats and ships that ran thousands of miles without suffering engine breakdowns. But when I became a pilot I soon learned some ships are subject to engine and equipment failures much more often than I realized. Some of them break down several times in just a few hours.

During one thirty day period in the Panama Canal I was the pilot aboard three ships that experienced major equipment failures. One ship lost the entire plant, engine, steering, lights and generators, all in a matter of seconds. Luckily I managed to get both anchors down and stop the ship forty feet short of a nearby bank. The steering aboard a second ship jammed hard right. The only thing that saved the ship from going aground was full astern on the engine causing the vessel to veer away from a nearby island. Aboard a third ship the steering also jammed hard over, and once again dropping both anchors saved the ship from hitting the rocks.

Just recently I was aboard a ship whose engine was computer controlled. In a six hour period between the dock and the pilot station, the ship had a complete breakdown twice. In addition there were steering failures three times while the ship was running full ahead. Also for two hours we steered without a compass, using nearby points of land to head on. Fortunately it was daylight. **It is necessary to point out that any small boat cruising nearby could have quickly been wiped out as the ship sheered off course without warning during these failures!**

2—**Bridge Orders to the Engine Room** — At some time in the past I am sure you have seen an engine room telegraph proudly displayed in a museum or a waterfront restaurant which previously had graced the bridge of some ship. If you stopped and studied this brass bound art work for a moment you noticed the round face of the telegraph was marked off in sections with the words **Dead Slow Ahead, Slow Ahead, Half Ahead,** and **Full Ahead,** all printed in big letters on one half of the face; and **Dead Slow Astern, Slow Astern, Half Astern,** and **Full Astern,** on the second half. This telegraph like others does not by itself start or stop a ship's engine, or even make it run faster or slower for that matter. It merely signals to the engineer below in the engine room, standing on the maneuvering platform, the speeds desired by the person in charge on the bridge. In the past as the ships have steamed by, you may have wondered just what are the various speeds that might be signaled on the engine room telegraph? To answer your query let us examine the signal **Dead Slow Ahead** for a moment. Depending on the ship, it could be any speed from 4.5 knots aboard a tired old bulk carrier up to 9.0 knots aboard a fast fruit boat carrying a load of bananas. . . . Surprised at the 9.0 knots, aren't you? In other words, the ship running at its slowest speed of 9.0 knots is running faster than most private boats do at full speed. **This raises the distinct possibility that if you are not alert, an over-taking ship even at dead slow ahead could run over you.**

The speed range of different types of ships can vary to a great degree, from slow to very fast. A look at the table below confirms this.

BULK CARRIER			BANANA BOAT
DEAD SLOW AHEAD (Manuevering)	=	4.5 knots	9.0 Knots
SLOW AHEAD (Manuevering)	=	8.0 Knots	12.0 Knots
HALF AHEAD (Manuevering)	=	10.0 Knots	15.0 Knots
FULL AHEAD (Manuevering)	=	12.0 Knots	18.0 Knots
SEA SPEED	=	15.0 Knots	23.0 Knots

Note the **Full Ahead** shown in the above table (Maneuvering and Sea Speed range). The modern diesel has two modes of operation—the **Maneuvering Mode** and the **Sea Speed Mode.**

The operating phase of the engine in any ship is the Maneuvering Mode. As a guide for the pilot's use there is posted somewhere on the bridge of every ship a Maneuvering Table showing the shaft revolutions, and the resulting speeds they produce. The table below is typical.

MANEUVERING TABLE		
DEAD SLOW AHEAD	45 RPM	5.9 KNOTS
SLOW AHEAD	60 RPM	7.8 KNOTS
HALF AHEAD	75 RPM	9.8 KNOTS
FULL AHEAD	90 RPM	11.8 KNOTS

As long as the engine speed is kept within the range of the RPM's shown in the Maneuvering Table the engine can be changed to run ahead or stern at a moment's notice. **Not true in the Sea Speed Mode! Beware! Ninety percent of the ships you meet will be running in the Sea Speed Mode.**

As I mentioned earlier, a large marine engine has no clutch. If while running ahead, it becomes necessary to put the engine astern, the engine must be stopped. The cam shaft is shifted and a powerful blast of air shot to the engine, causing it to turn over. This makes the pistons fire. The weakness in this system *is the blast of air.* It must be able to turn over the weight of the engine and its connecting shaft and propeller; but if the flow of water pressing against the propeller blades is too **strong**, the air blast cannot overcome the additional tons of Water/Weight pressing against the propeller. This being true, it follows that if the ship is moving through the water at a rapid rate of speed, the air blast is just not powerful enough to start the engine running from a stop position. The direct and immediate results: **A failed engine start equals a vessel out of control!** *Warning!!* **A ship out of control is a runaway giant likely to turn in any direction without notice. A decided danger to a nearby smaller vessel!**

When I was in the Panama Canal if an investigation was held concerning an accident, the first question asked and studied by the Inspection Board: "Was the vessel out of control?" The obvious answer: "Yes." "Yes" because the ship had struck some object and was not stopped in time to avoid an accident, thus out of control! In many cases out of control is not due to pilot error but because the engine failed or the steering malfunctioned.

Isn't it interesting, that of all craft moving over the face of the earth, only the water craft cannot be stopped quickly and efficiently. All land vehicles including airplanes setting down on runways are fitted with brakes to slow the craft and finally bring it to a stop. Not so a ship, as any of you know who own and pilot your own boat. I have seen the time when backing the engine has caused a collision with a nearby object due to the twisting of the hull under the torque of the turning propeller. This torque is quite apparent aboard vessels fitted with a right hand turning propeller which causes the stern of the vessel to move rapidly to port. For a pilot there is no more terrifying sound in the world than standing on the wing of the bridge, desperately needing a start, to hear nothing but blast after blast of air shot to the engine without results.

The point to this story is: If you in a small boat get close to any motor ship underway remember: **That lumbering elephantine ship cannot always be stopped by backing the engines even if it is necessary and vital to do so to save your life!**

Chapter Two

Maneuvering Large Ships Around Small Boats

Avoiding a collision on the water between a ship and a smaller boat involves two important factors. One is timing, the other speed. The pilot aboard the ships you meet is without doubt well aware of the maneuvering characteristics of your boat, whether it be sail or power driven. The pilot will know, not because he has been aboard your craft and had taken it out for a spin one sunny day, but because over the years he has observed thousands of boats moving through the pilotage area over which he is licensed to serve. Unless you are a pilot you are at a disadvantage because you know little or nothing about the maneuvering capabilities of a ship.

A ship is the most unruly vehicle ever conceived and built by the hand of man. The aircraft may experience similarities such as the effects of wind upon its path of travel, but the ship suffers the additional influence of water current. Often the water will flow from several directions with great force in only a short distance. Over the years it has been proven that electronic machines can be programed to assist or even do the work of the airplane pilot, except when heavy weather sets in, or an engine quits or the tail falls off. This is not true about ships.

The Panama Canal Company studied long and heard on how to replace the canal pilot. The study only proved it could not be done. The canal officials learned early, a computer called a human brain is the only instrument capable of putting a ship through the locks successfully. In other words shiphandling and maneuvering cannot be programed to off-

8

set the wind and currents that act upon the ship, at least not until some time after the forces have already come into play and affected the ship's direction of movement. By the time an electronic machine determines the ship has been affected, it is already too late to save the ship from doing damage in close quarters.

1—Steering and Engine Failures in Front of Ships — As a pilot I have wondered time and again why a boat stopped dead in the water near the path of a ship would, when the ship came close, suddenly start the engine and steer across the bow of the ship, only to stop and drift close by as the ship steamed past. Or why a fast boat would overtake a ship only a few feet away, then a short distance beyond, suddenly put the rudder over and cross the path of the ship. Numerous times they were so close I lost sight of them under the bow. Or why a private boat on a clear day will come at a ship head and head and never change course until under the bow. It totally confuses me why a person would play chicken with something as large and cumbersome as a ship. Bear this in mind. **While that person is playing chicken with the ship, it may well be a game played by him alone. For one reason or another, the pilot may not even see the boat.** Please believe I do not mind in the least changing course to clear a small boat. After all, that is my business. What does frighten me and every pilot is: suppose the boat dashing about loses steering suddenly, or the boat cutting across has an engine failure? In that case, **the ship by itself cannot avoid running over the smaller boat.** That's a nightmare I hope never to experience. Let me tell you a tale.

While I was a pilot in the Panama Canal I saw a small boat traveling fast in clear weather hit the side of a ship. On this particular day the visibility was unrestricted with a bright sun shining. The ship I was aboard had just left Gatun Locks on the Atlantic side of the Canal and was headed southbound toward the Pacific. My ship was in a line of five ships all maintaining a distance apart of approximately one mile. The column of ships had just cranked on full speed and was steering at fifteen knots when up ahead from around the bend in the channel there appeared an expensive boat traveling at

9

well over thirty knots. I can only surmise that the operator wanted to get a closer view of the ships because he hauled over and skimmed down the side of the lead ship. Then he passed the second ship, while all the time waving at the people on deck as he whizzed past.

Suddenly the boat turned sharply and dove straight into the side of the third ship in line. Fortunately the man driving the boat was alone at the time. Upon impact, with no seat belt to hold him, the operator went sailing out of the cockpit over the windshield. His body hit the ship's side only a second after the bow of the boat. He managed to hang on to the deck of his sinking craft. The thrashing propeller of the ship just missed the seriously damaged boat. Aboard my ship I quickly altered course to avoid running over the drifting wreck.

A Panama Canal boat was nearby repairing a buoy. The crew sped over to pick the poor devil from the boat seconds before it sank like a rock. I later read the Panama Canal Company investigation that the steering gear aboard the speed boat had jammed. The captain spent several weeks in the hospital recovering from a concussion, a broken arm and three cracked ribs. The point I am trying to make in telling of these two incidents is: a large ship, due to its size, weight, momentum and limited maneuverability, is often unable to get out of the way of a smaller and more handy boat if the commander either deliberately or by accident places his craft in a close and dangerous situation. It is an inescapable fact: **a smaller boat will, in *every* collision, come off second best!**

Common sense will tell the captain of a smaller boat that he has an enormous advantage over the ship when it comes to being able to stop quickly. He can turn to a new heading, or even turn completely around in a matter of seconds when necessary to save his life. **This quick maneuverability is not a privilege enjoyed by the pilot of a ship!**

Chapter Three
Visibility

1—Visibility from the Bridge of a Ship — I tell you here and now an unfortunate fact—**visibility from many ships is not good!** This is especially so of cargo ships with booms and masts sticking up like a forest before the wheelhouse windows. Cargo ships are cursed with a dozen to thirty or forty blind spots between the bridge and the bow.

Other cargo ships are fitted with large block type cargo cranes. Many bulk carriers are fitted with box-like affairs that travel up and down the main deck on railroad tracks. Both types can blind the pilot.

Aboard cargo ships with large amounts of cargo gear sticking up between the bow and the bridge, I have spent six hours walking rapidly from one side of the ship to the other in an effort to keep the area before the ship under constant observation. It would frighten you to tell the number of times I have thought the area before the ship was clear of small boats, only to shift my position on the bridge and discover a craft ahead that until a moment before had escaped my searching eyes. The boat had been concealed behind one or more pieces of cargo gear.

Keep one thing in mind as you venture out at night into the shipping lanes: the ships passing by at a high speed **do not slow down due to darkness!**

On the bridge of these ships two radar sets are in operation. One is watched over by the pilot. The other set is guarded by the mate on watch. These sets can be tuned to pick up almost any target in the area. The key word here is **almost**. It is a sad truth that once in a while a boat will not appear on the radar screen until the ship is almost upon the poor soul. There have

11

been instances where I picked out the port and starboard running lights of an approaching small craft long before it showed as a faint dot of light on the radar screen. Other times the radar failed to produce a target with the results that I almost ran down a small craft. My advice: **do not depend on the ship to pick up your boat by radar after dark either in fair weather or foul!**

2—**Darkness** — A condition we are all familiar with and adapt to in our everyday lives because we have electric lights. Turn off this ilumination after dark and each of us becomes instantly disadvantaged. Think back to the last time there was a sudden power failure at night. Remember how those around you groped to find a flashlight or a candle to light the way. This groping about is very much like going out on the water in a vessel after dark. There are few lights to brighten the path and highlight the dangers. Out on the water there may be only some faraway lighthouse. Its rays mark a distant location. However, today's modern ships ranging in size from the fast container ship cutting through the water at twenty three knots, to a small Japanese fishing boat plugging along at ten knots, do not grope in the dark. Each have an aid to light their way through the blackness of night. I refer to the radar, an instrument many private boats do not carry.

3—**Fog** — You have no doubt at some time been caught out on a cruise when the fog set in. Immediately you wished you were somewhere else. I am sure you knew the rules of the road, and blew all the proper signals. Even though you couldn't see, you had a pretty good idea of how to get back to where you started, or how to forge ahead to your destination. But did you know what to do when the first distant sound of a ship's fog horn reached your sensitive ears? If you are like most of us, you hoped and prayed the ship was not headed your way. As the sound of the whistle grew louder you finally determined this ghost ship was indeed coming in your direction. As the sound became louder and louder you began to wonder just what to do to avoid getting run over. Should you hold your course and speed? Should you slow down? Should you change the course? Maybe you should do both, slow down and change course? Perhaps you should turn around and go back from whence you came? Maybe it would be best to post an additional lookout and sound your fog horn more frquently. Being well versed in the rules of the road, you finally reduced the speed to bare steerage-way and began to pray when you realized the ship was in fact bearing down on your position. Most terrifying of all, you suspect the ship was traveling at a rate of speed greater than bare steerageway. As you heard the sound of other boats around you it was of little comfort to know the others were as helpless as yourself. Read on and I will tell you what to do in the future to avoid getting smashed and find yourself with nothing but little pieces of drift floating around in the ship's wake!

As you lived in fear, the pilot upon the bridge of the ship had his head buried in the radar and was wondering where in hell to go with the ship to find his way through several hundred small boats covering the radar screen. Meanwhile, behind him, the sound of the huge diesel engine pounds and thunders as it cranks out the miles, pushing the ship over the ground at hundreds of feet a minute. The pilot slows the huge engine to avoid the prospect of colliding at full speed with another vessel. Looking at the cluster on the radar screen, the pilot knows that all of the many targets before the ship are almost certain to be moving in different directions and at different speeds, some making only a few knots while others are travelling over thirty knots. Because the majority of the vessels are moving, the pilot is at a terrifying disadvantage in trying to steer the ship safely through the cluttered boats moving all over the screen.

In the fog when you first hear a ship's whistle in the distance you have a fairly certain idea of the direction from which the ship is approaching. However, as the ship draws closer the bearing of the sound will become defective due to the damp atmosphere.

When the ship is near your position it is most likely coming at you from an entirely different direction than you believe it to be from the sound. I cannot repeat it too often when I say: the sound of the powerful horn may seem to be coming at you from one direction when actually the ship is bearing down upon you from a surprising quarter! Know this always: as the

13

ship draws closer to your helpless craft it becomes more and more impossible for you to tell with any degree of assurance just what the true bearing of the ship might be! You might ask how I know this to be so? I know because I have been out in the fog aboard tugboats smaller than some of the private boats I see today, and this has happened to me. What should you do? Very simple. **Stop your craft dead in the water.** Now let me explain why I recommend this action on your part.

Long before the ship gets close you can be sure the pilot on board an approaching ship has you spotted on the radar screen, and every other small boat in your vicinity. Knowing where you are in relation to the ship, and provided you don't move, he can easily steer the ship around your position. But if you are underway, he must try and make allowances of where you will be at the time the two of you meet. Think about it for a moment. If a majority of the other vessels go in first one direction, then the other, it becomes one big crap shoot. If every boat runs about trying to escape the approaching ship's whistle the pilot on the bridge is up against a rapidly changing meeting, passing and over-taking situation involving many boats.

Forget for a moment the rules of the road and who has the right of way, which vessel must sound which signal, etc. The fact is, from a point of survival, and to avoid being run down, you are well advised to *stop your craft.* The pilot will steer around you. Let the other guy run about placing himself in danger. You do the sensible thing and stay in one spot. **After the ship is gone you can go on your way, and go on living!**

I remember some years ago when a friend of mine told me the story of a fast moving cabin cruiser ramming into the side of a ship on which he was serving as pilot during heavy fog. The ship was a huge vessel, measuring just under a thousand feet long. The ship was on a southerly course. Like all ships with excellent radar sets on the bridge, the ship was steaming at a reduced but good turn of speed. It was a summer morning, and as usual the radar screens were filled with hundreds of bright dots of light, each representing a boat of some type. Off to the starboard side the radar screen showed a large clear area free of contacts. However, before too long, a target two miles away from the opposite side of the clear area began to move toward the ship. The mate on watch, using the Radar Collision Avoidance System, began tracking what soon proved to be a fast moving target. In less than a minute it was determined this target was on a collision course and closing on the ship at twenty five knots, steering due east. Aboard the ship the engines were placed on stop and then backed down. The target continued closing and shortly was upon the ship. During this time there was nothing the ship could do by itself to avoid a collision. At this point, with nothing more to be done, the captain and the pilot rushed out to the starboard wing of the bridge and from over one hundred feet up in the air peered over the side of the ship.

Out in the fog they could hear boat engines go into reverse. A second later a power cruiser hit the ship. Upon impact, at approximately fifteen knots, the boat literally bounced back eight or ten feet away from the high steel wall of the ship's side, its bow stove in above the water line. The cabin cruiser still rolled due to the sudden stop and its captain appeared on deck unhurt and very angry. As his boat drifted down the side of the ship he spied the anxious captain and pilot peering over the side of this monstrous ship. At this he began cursing the two aboard this ship of fools who had deliberately steered a large ship into his path. When the pilot hollered down to ask if his craft was still seaworthy, the cruiser captain replied in very colorful language that it was. With that answer he went back inside, cranked up the engine and once again set off at top speed, disappearing into the thick fog. I tell this story to point out: **at times a large ship is a helpless creature when it comes to avoiding a small boat!**

An important fact to keep in mind is that a very limited number of ships enjoy the *luxury* of a Collision Avoidance System as shown on page 16, or a True Motion Radar set. The set found on most ships is a Relative Motion radar. This means all targets shown on the radar set move across the screen on a Relative Movement Line. Because of this fact it is impossible for a pilot to know your course and speed without working out a Vector Diagram Plot. In the fog, with several hundred

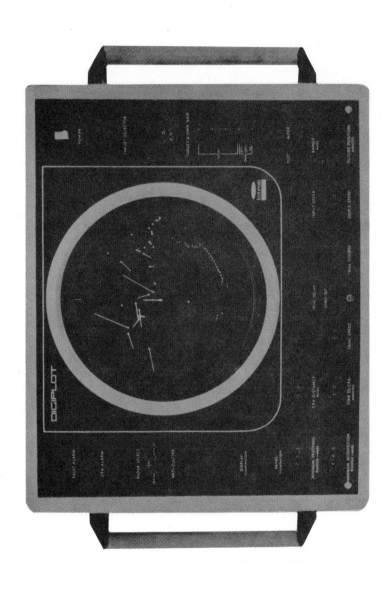

16

targets showing, the pilot does not have time to do a Vector Plot on each and very target.

Remember, while in the fog you are traveling toward the ship on a Relative Movement Line. In other words, you are moving across the radar screen with no way for the pilot to know which direction you are steering, or at what speed. Unfortunately you and the ship are both traveling in an information vacuum without knowing the other vessel's course and speed. But most important of all, *without knowing the other vessel's intentions!*

4—Rain — Just as in the case of darkness, the pilot depends on the radar during rain as one of the main sources of information to pinpoint the location of other vessels. Again the radar has limitations. Unfortunately, rain, like any other physical object, can be picked up by the radar and show like any other target on the screen. This would be well and good if it ended at that. But the heavier the rain, the more the radar screen will become cluttered.

Targets near and far are obscured. Rain can block out the more important targets such as your boat. Rain can be so heavy at times that the radar screen is covered completely with nothing but rain clutter. Other objects cannot be observed. I have watched rain coming down in such volume the radar became completely useless. Keep in mind, if the radar is useless in heavy rain, *then a visual sighting of your boat may be impossible!*

Surprisingly, one of the most deceiving types of rain is a light mist that drifts down out of the sky like a feather. This kind of rain can very effectively cover the radar screen and block out any and all objects, even the ones close by.

Beware, when it is raining there is no assurance that the ship will spot you on radar in time to avoid running you down! About the only advice I can give you, and it's not much, is: keep your eyes and ears open in any type of rain. And stay out of the shipping lanes as much as possible!

5—Color of your boat — Discounting how shipshape and squeaky clean a white boat may appear, white is the world's worst color to paint a small boat. It is very often hard to see from any distance. Too often white boats match with and blend into the sky. White fades into the atmosphere and blends with smoke and haze like a drifting ghost. Often it is difficult to see across the very water it floats in. During World War II the United States Navy had to issue special tinted sun glasses to navy carrier pilots. These glasses would highlight white when viewed from a distance over vast expanses of water. **If I owned a boat I would paint it any color but white.** One of the most vivid colors that can be seen over the water is red, with orange a close second. Some steamship companies paint their ships red, orange or blue for the simple reason these colors can be seen sooner and farther away through fog, rain and reduced visibility.

6—**Radar reflectors and your boat** — The large buoys you see today marking the channels and shoals make excellent targets for the radar for the most part. However, some of these only show as weak and fuzzy targets because they do not carry radar reflectors. This can also be said about some of the boats I meet during my transits between the pilot station and the docks. I am sure you have some type of radar reflector to hoist to the top of the mast during periods of reduced visibility. It is an excellent idea and one every sensible commander will follow. If the United States Coast Guard goes to all the time, trouble and expense to install radar reflectors on their navigational buoys, why should't the captain of a private boat take a page from the Coast Guard and do likewise? **Your best protection in fog and during darkness is to have a radar reflector!**

Chapter Four
Lights

When you drive your car at night, the best and most reliable form of protection you have against being hit by another moving chunk of iron is your car lights front and back. This is true many times over aboard your own craft when out on the water in the dark of night. There is no better protection offered, or precaution taken to avoid being run over than to pay as much attention to your boat lights as you do your car lights. It is vital for your safety to be seen early and at a great distance. To make sure of this, burn lights that show clearly and with brightness. This not only calls attention to your position, but just as important, your direction of travel. To write what is so obvious is almost embarrassing. But if you knew the thousands of times I have almost run down a smaller vessel because the lights were dim or badly placed it would scare you to death. I might add, smaller craft are not the only vessels running with poor lights. The list includes ships, barges under tow, fishing boats, naval craft and seaplanes. Tugboats are the exception. I have yet to see a tugboat without well placed bright lights.

If you are in doubt about how effectively your boat lights show, particularly when bright shore lights are burning in the background, you are not alone. When I went to sea, every vessel I sailed aboard, in charge of the watch, or responsible for its safe navigation, I attempted to determine at just what distance another vessel could see my lights. But how do you find out? A simple test I used years ago when sailing aboard tugs may help you. When moored in the harbor at night aboard a tug I was not familiar with, I would take a walk away from the dock, leaving the tug's navigation lights burning. During this walk I moved about in the area until the tug was in a position silhouetted against bright shore lights. Looking at the tug's lights told me clearly to what extent the lights aboard my tugboat could be seen by other vessels underway. It never ceased to amaze me how dim those bright lights aboard the tug became once I was some distance away. A like examination of your lights will certainly give you a clue as to how others see your lights.

You probably already know the lights of ships are hard to pick up at times, even during conditions of good visibility. **If this is true of ships—it is even more so with smaller vessels!**

Years ago when I sailed out of Seattle harbor aboard ocean-going tugboats towing large barges at night I used to turn on all the outside work lights on deck. I hoped the inbound ships coming into Seattle harbor would use them as a guide to quickly pick out my cluster of towing lights against the hundreds of city lights blazing behind me.

Now after years of piloting I know even the extra deck lights were not always effective. Given these facts, what chance does a small craft stand to be seen by the pilot of a ship at night? **Not good! The odds are not in your favor!**

 1—**Crossing and Meeting** — When checking the brightness of your lights from a distance you might also check to see if the red port light can be seen across the starboard bow, or the green starboard light can be seen across the port bow. Aboard a ship meeting your craft at night, if the beam of either the red or green light can be seen across the wrong bow, it is a serious problem. Many times I have been unable to determine if a small boat I was meeting was steering a course to clear my vessel by a safe margin because of its bum misplaced sidelights. This has happened so often, now anytime I meet a small boat at night I am uneasy until I have determined with certainty if I will clear the on-coming boat. When meeting a ship at night to avoid a problem concerning just what direction you are really heading—**Change course to a large angle—the pilot will then have no doubt about what direction you are heading!**

20

2—Distances between the white navigation lights aboard extra large ships. — In the days when the biggest vessels afloat were the battleships, the distance and spread between the white navigation lights of vessels really didn't matter too much because the ships were small. However, in today's world as the ships grow bigger and longer (some longer than the Empire State Building is tall), the distance between the ship's forward white masthead light and the white after range light becomes quite significant to the commander of smaller vessels. These two lights placed one at the bow and the other in the vicinity of the stern aboard very large vessels are spaced so far apart the commander of a smaller craft navigating close to the surface of the water may have trouble recognizing these two lights as belonging to the same vessel.

To bring some perspective to just how long a ship can actually be I would like to quote from a newspaper, the *Seattle Times*—the title of the piece was, "Ship is man's biggest machine." "Oranges and apples shouldn't be compared, as buildings and ships shouldn't, but bear with me."

Maybe you read about it in the Times Sunday—the biggest building, 76 stories, west of Chicago and north of Houston to be built in Seattle.

It will be named the Columbia Center, 954 feet tall—half again taller than the 609 foot Seafirst building. Impressive all right.

But I have a pet saying: The biggest moving machine that man ever built is a ship—was historically and still is. You may recall the giant SL-7 containerships that called here until a few months ago. They were 964 feet long.

Remember that I used to say if one were stood on end it would reach higher than the Seafirst building? Stand an SL-7 on end and it will out-reach the 954-foot-high Columbia Center from ground level. Navy aircraft carriers are even longer. Now class is dismissed and no quiz today. . . .

—Reprinted by permission of *The Seattle Times.* Copyright 1982.

At every chance, study the bigger ships and understand how during darkness the distance between the white lights can appear to be unconnected. There have been documented cases of good-sized craft whose captains failed to realize two widely spaced white lights were at the bow and stern of one ship. Trying to make passage between them brought disaster. The captain failed to realize there was a ship's hull between the two lights.

3—**Overtaking** — One of the most dangerous spots you as the captain of a smaller craft can find yourself in at night is to be in front of a ship traveling in the same direction as yourself. The first hint of danger will come when the ship is close aboard and towering over you like a mountain. If that happened to you in the past, the pilot did not deliberately steer to run you down. You may have thought so at the time when you heard the big bow wave crashing and curling on itself just over your shoulder. The chances are excellent the pilot did not pick you up visually, by radar, or the bow lookout failed to see you. Maybe the officer on watch did not catch you in his binoculars because your boat was obscured behind a piece of rigging aboard the ship. There could be many reasons too numerous to mention. The most common reason is a weak burning stern light aboard your boat. Over the years I have observed thousands of weak stern lights aboard small craft which could not be seen more than a half mile away. To the pilot aboard a ship this distance is nothing. Think on this for moment; if your vessel is located one half a mile ahead of a ship and making eight knots, and the ship behind is steaming at fifteen knots, the ship is coming up your stern at a speed of seven knots. At seven knots, and a distance of one half mile, the ship has to only run four minutes until it is climbing aboard your craft as an unwanted guest.

As a pilot, one of the most apprehensive periods for me is during the night when I am overtaking a vessel and there is no communication. Private boats fall into this area.

Hundreds of times a year aboard ships it becomes necessary for me to come up astern and overtake smaller vessels at a very close range, sometimes less than a ship's length away. At night it is my fear the boat ahead will not be aware of my presence and suddenly turn in front of the ship. Every pilot is aware the person in the boat just ahead may not be the captain, and can be in a state from alert to tired, to sleepy, or even drunk. God forbid. It has happened to every pilot. A boat ahead has been mis-navigated, and quickly turned into the path of his ship, leaving the pilot little time to react. Allow me to tell another true story from tugboat days on runs back and forth to Alaska.

In the fall of 1958 I was serving in a big ocean-going tug towing a large chemical barge between Seattle and Alaska. The barge was wide as a World War II Liberty Ship. Occasionally we towed it almost as fast. At the time I was first mate with many trips to my credit up and down what is called the Inside Passage to Alaska. We had delivered our cargo of chemicals to the pulp mill up north and were heading back south, looking forward to arriving home. We didn't know people were going to die under our barge before we entered our home port.

It was a black night as only it can be in the north country when we entered one particularly long and beautiful stretch of water known the world over as Grenville Channel. Many of you have probably sailed through it. The passage at one point narrows to less than a mile wide, with a depth of water several hundred feet deep right up to the shore. In effect, Grenville Channel is a deep open-ended canyon filled with water that swiftly flows through it as the tide ebbs and flows. Mountains covered with lush forests tower into the sky from the banks like silent sentinels guarding the ages. Along the shore the branches of the trees hang over the channel and have been known to sweep the decks of passing vessels.

About four thirty in the morning this particular trip during the second mate's watch, we were in the narrowest part of the channel and over-taking three fishing boats. Two boats were on the port and one on the starboard side, and all spaced approximately one mile apart. Our tug over-took the two boats on the port hand safely. However, the boat on the starboard bow cut sharply to the left when abeam and almost hit the tug. Quick action by the second mate in turning the tug's bow away saved the two vessels from a collision. Immediately the man in the wheelhouse of the fishing boat, apparently confused by all the lights of the tug sweeping by, stopped the engine close under the stern of our tug. This was unfortunate because the fishing boat quickly caught the full brunt of the tug's powerful propeller wash and was rapidly forced back directly under the bow of the barge eight hundred feet astern.

The fishing boat was now helpless to do anything, and found itself lying across the huge anchor chain towing bridles. The forty five foot boat was in effect being towed broadside through the water at nine and a half knots, while all the time filling with tons of cold sea water.

The tragic results of this over-taking situation: the man steering was swept out of the wheelhouse and to this day his body never found. A man sleeping below in the bow was trapped by the water pouring in and drowned. His body was later removed in the shipyard. The only one out of a crew of three to survive was the captain sound asleep in his cabin behind the pilothouse.

To this day I will never forget running out on deck in my night clothes and looking back to see in the glare of our powerful searchlight the sight of a large white fishing boat impaled in our towing gear as the barge charged down the channel plowing up the water.

The question: what can be done in the future to prevent this from happening to other poor souls aboard unfortunate craft? It might be yourself in the wrong set of circumstances. The facts as they exist on our waterways today are limited, sorry to say.

When fast moving commercial and privately owned craft fill our inland waters to overflowing, when expensive ships (some costing over $50,000 per day to operate) hurry to meet stevedore gangs standing by to unload costly cargo onto waiting freight trains, when fast ships rush to fill thousands of trucks needed to carry the goods down our nation's highways, when tugs and barges are pulling hard to beat the changing tide, when ferry boats hurry to met the posted schedules, it only means you, the private boat captain, are at an enormous disadvantage when caught up in this frenzy of activity. And all you wanted was to have a good time.

What can you do to protect yourself from a rapidly advancing large ship bent on coming so close you can hear and feel the thunder of the powerful stroking engine pounding through the night like an iron chariot pulled by fiery steeds lashed on to ever greater speed? **Why not use a** *flare-up-light?*

4—Flare-up-light — Unfortunately the flare-up-light is very seldom employed by the captain of private vessel. Why, I never have understood. In fact, I have never seen the captain of a power boat use this important aid to safety. It is my guess the sailing ship commander, due to his limited speed and slow response in attempting to get out of the way, has learned to employ the flare-up-light flashed against the sail as a matter of survival.

I have always been thankful to the captain of a smaller craft who, on a dark night showed a flare-up-light as my ship bore down on his position. The only fault I find is the lights employed are not bright enough to be seen from a good distance.

However, in comparison, among the numerous criticisms I have about the equipment of the ships I climb aboard, is the lack of a search light to use as a flare-up-light. **Do not expect a flare-up-light to be flashed from a deep draft vessel!**

Right now you are asking: "What is a flare-up-light?" Quite simply, it is a tool and aid allowed to be used by all water craft under the rules of the road. The first time I saw a flare-up-light used consistently and successfully was up and down the Inside Passage to Alaska in the nineteen fifties. In those days when I made my way back and forth to Alaska towing all manner of barges, a number of cruise ships flying the Canadian flag plied those waters. They were fast, sleek vessels loaded to the gunwales with American tourists. The ships kept to a rigid schedule and very seldom slowed down, certainly not when over-taking the hundreds of fishing boats that ambled back and forth across the narrow channels all hours of the day and night. During darkness the captains and mates of those ships when coming up astern of any vessel, would switch on their powerful search light mounted high on the flying bridge. The rays of this light were then flashed all up and down the shore alongside the vessel they were over-taking. Believe me it was effective! When the beam of that massive light exploded the shore into daylight right alongside the poor unsuspecting person drowsing his time through the long night watch, that person knew two things instantly: one—someone was behind him who was coming through, and two—he had better pull over and make room. **That, my friend, was the flare-up-light supreme!**

For your best protection in the exercise of good seamanship I recommend the use of a bright flare-up-light at night by both sail and power boat if there is any doubt a ship bearing down on your position might not see you in the darkness. In the case of a power boat you may already have a searchlight which is excellent for this purpose. A point to consider when shopping around for a flare-up-light is: **A light of any size smaller than a five cell flashlight in candle power is very difficult to see from the bridge of a fast moving ship!**

Chapter Five

Crossing Ahead of a Ship

Have you ever driven your car down a long stretch of highway without another car in sight when suddenly a car pulled up to the side of the road at the intersection and came to a stop? As you continued toward this car at a high rate of speed you could clearly see the driver looking both ways to check the traffic before starting out to cross the road. At that point you knew, even though you were rapidly drawing closer, that the driver was going to zoom out in front of you. And he did. You just barely missed a collision because you slammed on the brakes to allow him or her room to go ahead.

Afterwards, in addition to being angry and frightened as you continued down the road, you perhaps fell to wondering why a person who had the intelligence to drive a car would place himself into such immediate danger. All he had to do was wait for a few seconds until you were safely past the intersection.

This very same thing has happened to me thousands of times aboard ships which are certainly many times heavier and bigger than any automobile ever built, and I can't figure why except I believe those commanders of approaching boats underestimate the speed and distance of an approaching ship. Any pilot of a large vessel can tell you a thousand stories of boats driving in front of his ship. So many near misses happen, pilots only shrug and put it in the back of their minds until it happens again.

Remember next time when starting across the bow of a ship some distance away, the ship is traveling fast and has no brakes to slam on to give you more room.

27

Thousands of times over the years private boats have run in front of my vessel. Most of these boats have been commanded by people who are known to have common sense, good judgment, and practice smart seamanship and courtesy of a high caliber. In recent years it has become more and more evident to me that captains of private boats have become acutely aware there is a real danger to their boats and the passengers on board when they navigate so close to the path of an up-coming ship. They force that ship to make a radical course change to avoid smashing into their craft. To a pilot, one of the more horrifying experiences is watching a smaller craft disappear from sight under the wide flaring bow of a ship underway. I have tried over the years to imagine the thought processes of the commander of a smaller craft who, from the stern of a sailing craft, or the flying bridge of a beautiful power boat, will watch an approaching vessel, certainly on a collision bearing, then steer his pride and joy directly into the path of the ship. I have often wondered what the view must be to that captain at the extreme point when the ship's bow towers like a huge cliff over his vessel only a few feet away. Just the noise of the crashing bow wave alone must be enough to strike terror into the bravest of hearts.

It may interest you to know when a small boat runs in front of a ship and gets in too close, the pilot on the ship will lose sight of the smaller vessel long before a point of impact can be reached. Once under the bow of the ship and out of sight the unfortunate boat captain is on his own to escape the death trap he finds himself in. The pilot, once he loses sight of the boat, dares not turn the ship because he does not know in what direction the boat commander may turn during the next few minutes. If the pilot does turn the ship he very possibly might turn it to the same direction the boat has turned. The results: **A smashed boat and possible death to those on board!**

Chapter Six
The Dance Of Death

When it comes to meeting other vessels, including ships, there is sometimes a happening I call the Dance Of Death. It is the same dance all of us at one time or the other have been involved in ashore when meeting another person in a hallway or perhaps on a sidewalk. I am sure each of you when meeting a stranger and trying to pass, have dodged to one side, only to have the other person also dodge in the same direction. Then as you dodge back the other way, so did the stranger. And all the time you were drawing ever closer, until finally one or both of you stopped and waited until it was clear who was going to go which way. Before this happened, maybe you even bumped into the other person.

I have observed and been involved in this same changing of direction when meeting or crossing with another vessel. First I change course, and no sooner done, than the other vessel will change course in the same direction. Then it's back and forth with each vessel changing course as a potential collision draws nearer. Today when that dance first starts I do a simple thing. I change course early and hold to it. To avoid this dance of death I have in the past even started out changing course and then finally turned completely around. I have even started steaming back in the direction from whence I had just come. Simply because one or more boats could not or would not decide what course to set and hold it until the ship had passed clear.

By this action of turning completely around, I in effect, said: "Let the other guy explain how he hit me in the stern." For all concerned it is extremely dangerous to change course continually in a crossing or meeting situation. Make one sensible and substantial course change early to clear the ship, and if at all possible stick with it. The key word here is *early*.

Chapter Seven

Why Will a Ship Hold Course Until Close to a Small Boat?

The answer to this question is one sought by the captains of many private boats right after they find themselves near a ship because the ship would not change course. Once again allow me to relate a short tale as to why a ship will do this: on a summer day about a year ago I was pilot aboard a roll on and roll off ship. This particular ship, almost eight hundred feet long and one hundred fifty feet wide, was streaking through the water at twenty four knots. Hundreds of boats were out on the water this beautiful day. I was weaving my way through boat after boat scattered out on each bow. The ship was in a hurry to make the dock before the stevedore gangs began their shift. The captain was standing by my side sipping coffee from a plastic cup and not saying a word. My orders to the helmsman and his response were given in low voices almost covered by the blowers of the air conditioner, and the grinding of the gears in the heavy radar antennas turning high on the mast above the bridge. The gyro compass repeater ticked off the degrees as the ship's head swung back and forth across the heading.

After a time, out on the port bow at a distance of three miles, a very fast power boat came toward the ship on a collision bearing. As I watched, the range closed until I could make out the details of the boat. I could see the captain looking at the ship. Finally he was close enough to be seen in larger detail but he continued hanging on to his course and speed. The seconds ticked by and still he kept on and kept on. At last I ordered a course change to the left, planning to pass astern. The order was no sooner spoken and the ship began to turn than the boat changed course. But to the right. Immediately I shifted the rudder and swung to the right leaving the boat out on my port hand.

The captain of the ship turned to me, laughing at my curse, and said. "John, you know better than to change course until you are about to swallow the poor fellow."

He paused before leaving the bridge. "I have seen it happen a thousand times. The other chap only changes course after the ship starts turning."

The captain threw his plastic cup into a nearby wastepaper basket. "You change course and the other fellow changes too, but to a more dangerous heading. **Unfortunately it is usually into the path of the ship!**"

1—Distances fore-lengthened and fore-shortened over the water — For years I wondered why a smaller vessel in a crossing or meeting situation, when the circumstances indicated the ship must hold its course because of the close proximity of other vessels or land, would wait so long to change its course and relieve a tight situation.

It wasn't until I had been a Panama Canal pilot for some months that I finally figured out one day why a person in a small boat would knowingly, willingly and deliberately navigate his craft in close to a ship underway. It has to do with two people's different conceptions of how much distance there is between two meeting vessels.

To the pilot aboard the ship high on the bridge with the wide decks of a ship spread out before him, **the distance to objects over the water is fore-shortened.** In other words, the distance to an object appears to be much less than it actually is.

Conversely to the captain of a smaller vessel, **the distance to objects over the water is fore-lengthened. In other words, the distance appears to be much greater than it actually is.** The diagram on page 32 illustrates this phenomenon.

How I became aware of this fact happened when, in the Panama Canal, I had to quickly learn just how to properly anchor a ship in a small, crowded anchorage filled to overflowing with numerous ships. The rule of thumb I learned to

PILOT'S VIEW—
WITH DISTANCE
FORE-SHORTENED

SMALL BOAT
CAPTAIN'S VIEW
FORE-LENGTHENED

32

use most effectively is this: **If the distance to a nearby anchored ship appears to be one ship length, the distance between the two ships is actually three times that, or three ship lengths.**

It is because of this fore-shortening effect that some pilots experience difficulty in placing a ship at a proper spot in an anchorage. More than one pilot has re-anchored a ship because the captain complained about the position once the anchor set up. The captain honestly believed the ship was anchored too close to the shore or another ship. Sometimes when a captain complains to me about being anchored too close I request he step into the shore launch with me as I leave the ship and look for himself. When the captain is in the launch and away from the ship he immediately recognizes that his vessel is indeed properly anchored with plenty of swinging room between other ships and the shore.

Keep in mind when you meet a ship close, the pilot on the bridge after a time becomes nervous about how near you are getting to his course, especially if other vessels are in the area and must be dealt with by the pilot if he is forced to change course.

Long before you think there is any real danger of being run over, remember: **For the pilot the distance to your vessel seems less than it really is, and to you the distance seems greater. This is a real conflict at a most critical juncture as you both rush toward each other. If you change course before you really think it necessary, you can only be safer.**

Chapter Eight
Wake of a Ship and the Bow Wave

The wake of a ship underway can be both deceiving and dangerous to a small boat, and most important, the ship doesn't have to run you down for its wake to cause great damage and even death under certain circumstances. If you think this statement is too dramatic and overstated please let me assure you it isn't. Consider this:

All ships underway produce two different wave actions. The first wave action is the wave thrown off to the side of the ship by the bow. It is the wave most obvious to the casual observer of a passing ship. It is the wave that curls away from the bow and spreads out as the ship cuts through the water with a bone in her teeth. It is easily recognizable because it is steep in shape, sharp in outline, and fans out from each side of the bow in the form of a V, after which it completely curls over, and breaks like a surf wave striking the beach. This is the wave most private boat captains see and curse as it rolls their vessel about spilling drinks and food. From my observation high on the ship, this is the wave all small boats deal with most effectively. Unfortunately there is a second wave just as uncomfortable and dangerous to the private boat.

From my own observation this second wave made by the ship is not apparent to the majority of small boats, and as a result they do little or nothing to avoid its power and force until it is too late. I refer to the stern wake or what some call the following wake. A following wake is usually unnoticeable to the small boat captain when looking at an approaching ship. This wave is really more of a swell. It is very large and packs a lot of power. It travels very fast. If the ship is

34

steaming at twenty two knots, this wake will also speed over the water at twenty two knots. It will travel at this speed a long distance after the ship has swept past.

A long time boating friend of mine and a very aware captain when it comes to safety told me that tugs running light without tows behind are also a big hazard. He told me they produce a swell big enough and steep enough to bury a good sized boat if caught. In one of his own instances his boat was almost wrecked as the result of a wave from a passing tug. He told me: "Just because a tugboat looks small it does not necessarily mean the wave and swell left behind is small."

The following wake, unlike the bow wave, is not just one wave but a series of deep swells that roll along evenly spaced. They are long, deep and resemble rolling hills and valleys. They remind me of the huge ground swells I used to observe at sea. The following wake does not break away from the side of the ship in a wide divergence. The following wake, like its name implies, follows the ship. From the bridge of the ship it can be seen following with the ship and traveling the same true course. Many of you from the Navy have been thrilled when you saw a destroyer steam by at a high rate of speed with an immense rooster tail towering above the stern. I am sure you were impressed with the size and power of such a wave. A lesser speed vessel does not produce such a spectacular sight but the wave it produces is never-the-less dangerous to a small boat, especially after the boat has just survived a large bow wave and is not prepared for the onslaught of the following waves that hit after the ship has passed.

Several hundred times each summer I watch with dread as small boats of all sizes and descriptions come near the stern of some fast container ship I am aboard, and shortly afterwards are almost swamped in the huge following waves. **They did not know these waves existed until it was too late and they were almost turned upside down!**

The following wake from a smaller ship is often more dangerous than from a large ship. I have navigated some of the biggest and fastest container ships running in the world today, and believe it or not they threw off such a slight bow and stern wave it was just about impossible to see these waves from the bridge. You ask me how I know there is only a slight wave by sight alone? Very simple. I have asked tugboat captains nearby to call me on the VHF radio and report the amount and size of the swell thrown off as I passed close aboard. Often they tell me if they had not seen the ship go by they would not have known about it because the swell was so slight it hardly moved the tug.

One of the biggest surprises to me when I first began to pilot large fast container ships was the speed of the ship versus the size of the swell. Like me, you probably believed the faster ship moves through the water, the bigger the waves and swell produced. *Not true!*

There is a type of ship eight hundred feet long and one hundred and five feet wide running regularly into my pilotage area. It travels between twenty two and twenty four knots, or even twenty seven with a good tidal current pushing it over the ground. In my area this ship will meet or overtake a number of tugboats with log rafts in tow. Each of these log rafts require a slow down by ships to reduce the swell size so as not to break the chains and gear holding the mass of logs together.

One day while southbound I rounded a rather blind bend and to my surprise a tugboat with a long log raft was sitting close under the point. With no time to drop the speed the ship rushed past and for the first time I had the opportunity to watch at close range the swells from this galloping machine sweep over a vulnerable raft of logs. The whole raft heaved and gyrated about in the rolling water like the mid-section of a belly dancer in full sway. Then a few months later I passed close by another log raft with the same ship. This time I had ample warning and was able to reduce the speed from twenty three knots to ten knots over the ground. To my great surprise the swell from the ship at this reduced speed caused a much greater movement over the log raft. I thought on this long and hard without coming to any firm conclusion until one day while watching hydroplane boat races on television, the reason hit me like a flash out of the blue.

Some ships, because of their under water shape coupled with fast speed, produce one type of swell size and shape, while the same hull at a slower speed throws out an entirely different swell, and one that can be much more destructive. At high speeds these ships plane through the water and climb up on what I call **the step**, just as a hydroplane racing boat at full power will do. Both the racing boat and the ship at high speeds squat by the stern, raise the bow and thus change the shape and amount of the hull passing through the water. This accounts for both vessels throwing off a less destructive swell at high speeds.

Before leaving the subject of ships' swells I would be greatly remiss if I did not mention ship swells that sweep ashore long after a ship has passed. Some of these swells are higher than a man's head, and can easily equal the power of an ocean surf. I have seen small boats drifting in close to a beach unaware that a ship's swell was about to bury the sandy beach in a cascade of foaming, boiling water. Too late the people in the boat realized they were in a heavy surf, and as a result had to struggle to avoid being swamped in the shallow water and large waves. **If you see a ship steaming past your area and you are close to the beach, keep a sharp lookout for the swell that is sure to arrive. Before it happens, put some distance between yourself and the shore!**

Chapter Nine

Cutting Ships Close Astern

For those craft who cut in close to the stern of a ship underway, there is not only the danger of the following wake but a danger of getting caught in the wheel wash. This propeller wash thrown out in back of a ship flows faster and is many times more powerful than any mountain river you have ever seen or heard roaring down a steep gorge. I have often wondered why a person who wouldn't launch his boat across a turbulent, swift-flowing river will deliberately and willfully steer across the stern of a fast moving ship whose forty thousand horsepower engine is pushing back a wide river of boiling water.

I have seen boats dangerously forced over onto their side to the point I believed they were going to ship water aboard and sink when caught in this powerful stream of water!

It is a complexing thing about this life we lead that similarly strange happenings take place almost together. Earlier I wrote about the fishing boat cutting in astern of our tugboat and winding up riding the chain towing bridles of our barge. This caused the death of two men by drowning. Almost the identical thing happened about a year later to a friend of mine, a captain aboard another tugboat towing a railroad car barge.

On this particular day the tug was northbound approaching Ketchikan, Alaska, with the barge trailing astern about 600 feet. It was a clear day in broad daylight when once again a fishing boat for an unknown reason deliberately cut between the tug and the barge. The captain of the fishing boat may have thought he could speed across the wake of the tug without mishap. How mistaken he was.

Just like the fishing boat cutting astern of our tug earlier, this fishing boat also wound up riding the chain bridles of a large sea-going barge. This time, however, the crew of a fishing boat were awake and alert and managed to escape to the open decks where they clung for dear life as dark green sea water boiled around them.

My skipper friend had the presence of mind to keep the tug pulling at full power, thus keeping a large portion of the fishing boat out of the water. Next he called the Coast Guard and requested they stand by in the harbor with several assist boats. Then off the city dock he gradually slowed the tug's engine until the barge was stopped and drifting. The Coast Guard boats pulled the helpless fishing boat clear of the under-slung shovel nose of the barge. The entire episode could have been avoided if the fishing boat captain had not acted in an un-seaman-like manner.

These two happenings graphically point out the propeller wash of any vessel is dangerous to a small vessel and once caught in it they cannot escape its clutches!

Chapter Ten

Suction Astern of the Ship

There is the additional danger of suction when cutting in very close to the stern of a ship traveling through the water. Perhaps a short story from the past will illustrate my point. Years ago the mate of a tug where I was serving as deckhand had a fine car. He was very proud of it and spent a great deal of time boasting about it. And well he should, it was indeed a beauty. He kept it washed and polished to a high gloss, and I believe he would have killed anyone who even touched it.

The thing he loved most about the car, more than its big size, configuration, luxury and name, was the high rate of speed he could attain with it, and the small amount of time he spent traveling between two points. In those days the fastest thing on the highway was the Greyhound bus. His plan of attack when barreling up the highway was to fall in behind one of these big land cruisers and slowly inch up to its back sides until he was only a few feet away from the massive bumper. At that point he would ease his foot off the gas pedal and from then on continue making the same high rate of speed up the road as he had been enjoying earlier. He burned a great deal less gasoline to do it. He was, of course, being pulled along by the air currents that suck forward and swirl in large eddies around the back end of the large bus. This same type of suction effect takes place in and around the water area of the propeller wash of a ship. It is true the propeller is throwing water astern, but it is also true there is a very large swirl of water at the top portion of the propeller wash that moves back forward. It can suck a small boat into the stern of a ship. The results can easily be damage to your craft or even sinking. **In other words, don't come too close and get sucked in over your head!**

Chapter Eleven
Ship's Rudder and Water Flow

Before the next chapter dealing with currents, it is a good time to talk about water flow passing the rudder of a ship underway, how it affects its efficiency, along with the subjects of advance and transfer, and the resulting danger to a small boat underway. Only one type of ship in the world I know of has the rudder located forward of the propeller, the submarine. All other ships have this barn door-like affair placed aft of the propeller to provide maximum control underway. Ninety nine percent of the ships you meet will be single propeller ships with a single rudder capable of being turned from (1) to (35) degrees to either side.

As you know, a ship underway is steered and held to a desired course because a large block of water moves over and around the rudder. To carry this thought a little farther, it is obvious the same block of water moves by the rudder whether the ship is traveling through the water at one or forty knots. The block of water never changes.

What does change when the ship is moving is the force of the water striking the rudder. This means when the engine is running at full speed, the propeller is also turning at maximum revolutions. This throws water against the rudder with great power and at a more rapid rate, which provides the ship with a quick turn rate and positive steering control. Reduce the power of the water hitting the rudder (slow the engine) and the turn rate of the ship's head will slow. Thus there is a reduction in positive steering control. Next, stop the engine and propeller from turning and the ship, in a very short time, will be slow to turn and sluggish in its movements. Stop the propeller from turning long enough and the ship will eventually be impossible to steer in a straight line.

The danger for you comes when you are close to a ship underway at full speed and that ship is forced to suddenly slow down or, worse, stop its engine. The water power to the rudder is gone and the speed of the water flow is reduced which leads to a loss of steering, in effect, *the ship is out of control.*

The subject of water flow past the ship's rudder is taught to every Panama Canal pilot during his training period. Once again here is a story from the Panama Canal about water flow and rudders. There is a spot in the Panama Canal named Bohio Turn. It is located eight miles south of Gatun Locks on the Atlantic side. During a transit of the canal it is one of the sharpest and shortest turns made by a Panama Canal pilot. It requires a course change of sixty degrees in less than one quarter of a mile. One day some years ago a very large and well known passenger ship was traveling the canal northbound. As this huge ship loaded with over a thousand passengers and crew approached Bohio Turn the pilot in charge kept the ship running at full speed. Every pilot-in-training in the Panama Canal is told over and over again to drop the engine rpms to at least half speed while still some distance away from this sharp turn. But why drop the speed before starting the turn, you ask? Very simple: it is to reduce the speed of the ship through the water and reduce the flow of water passing the rudder before starting the turn. Then if the ship fails to turn fast enough, merely increase the engine rpms, which forces more water against the rudder. This results in a faster turning ship in a shorter distance traveled.

At any rate on this particular day the pilot, when part way through the turn at full speed, knew the ship was not turning quickly enough to clear the rapidly approaching land directly ahead and close to the ship. Unfortunately, because the ship was running flat out with the four churning propellers eating up the distance like a devouring monster, there was nothing he could do at that point to prevent the ship from grounding. The result: considerable damage to the ship.

As shown by the above story, if you get in front of a ship running underway at full speed, and the ship starts a sharp turn in an attempt to avoid you (and it seems the ship is not turning fast enough to do so), **the ship cannot increase the rate of swing! You will have to move your own vessel to escape!**

An interesting footnote to rudders and water flow is if a pilot is forced into a position where for some reason he cannot reverse the engine after it is stopped, and he wishes to reduce the speed through the water, there is a method to accomplish this: rapid shift the rudder from hard right to hard left numerous times until the ship is slowed to a desired speed. Believe me it works. The rudder flopping from side to side is a heavy drag for a ship to carry through the water. The effect is similar to a parachute dragging from the back end of a fast jet landing on a short runway. This action will also turn the ship's hull away from the direction of travel because in effect each time the rudder is put over, the hull turns slightly and starts to slide sideways. A huge piece of steel moving broadside through the water even at a small angle will not long maintain a high rate of speed.

If you find yourself in tight quarters with a failed engine you might have some success in slowing your craft down to a more comfortable speed by performing this trick used by pilots.

1—Advance — The problem the pilot of the passenger ship in Bohio Turn came up against in addition to water flow past the rudder had to do with what is known among pilots as **advance** and **transfer.** Because you are probably not familiar with the term, let me explain with a drawing I received from the captain of a large container ship.

A ship running at full speed (and most you meet are) has a maximum flow of water constantly passing the rudder, thus producing top steering performance. But when this vessel at full speed starts to swing, the ship will continue to **advance** in the same direction the vessel was moving before the turn was started. This is called **advance.**

It is plain from the diagram on the following page that the vessel at full speed, after starting a turn, will move ahead

MANEUVERING CHARACTERISTICS

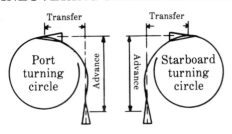

TURNING CIRCLE

		Full Load Condition			Ballast Condition		
		Advance	Transfer	Time	Advance	Transfer	Time
Full Speed	Port	2,350	1,300	1 - 25	2,200	1,000	1 - 15
	Starboard	2,400	1,300	1 - 30	2,250	1,150	1 - 15
Half Speed	Port	1,900	1,050	2 - 20	1,650	700	1 - 55
	Starboard	1,950	1,050	2 - 25	1,700	750	2 - 00

DISTANCE AND TIME REQUIRED TO STOP VESSEL
(when full astern operated) (90 RPM)

	Full Load Condition		Ballast Condition	
	Distance	Time	Distance	Time
Full Speed	9,600	7 - 40	6,600	5 - 20
Half Speed	2,000	3 - 40	1,550	2 - 50

Distances are in feet, time in minutes and seconds

RPM vs Speed (Knots)

		Full Load Condition		Ballast Condition	
	Load	RPM	Speed	RPM	Speed
	Normal	122	23.0	122	24.0
	70 MR	112	21.5	112	22.0
	50 MR	101	19.5	100	19.5
Harbor	Full	60	12.0	60	12.0
	Half	50	10.0	50	10.0
	Slow	40	8.0	40	8.0
	D. Slow	30	6.0	30	6.0

	Full Load	Ballast
Disp.	35,480	20,180
Draft	31' 03"	19' 09"
Trim	0	9' 01"
Full Speed	23.0	24.0
Half Speed	12.0	12.0

WARNING!
The response may be different from those listed above if any of the following conditions, upon which the maneuvering information is based are varied.
1. Calm weather—Wind 10 knots or less, calm sea.
2. No current
3. Water depth greater than twice the vessel's draft
4. Clean hull
5. Clean hull and clean propeller

some 2,350 feet (almost half a land mile) before coming to a new heading ninety degrees from the original course.

2—Transfer — To talk about **advance** without mentioning TRANSFER is impossible. Once again, referring to the diagram on page 44, we see that transfer is the distance the ship will travel at right angles to the original course after the turn is started. I would like to point out the distance of transfer as shown by the diagram is half the distance of advance. This is called drag, explained next.

The hull of every vessel, no matter what size, is designed to make the best speed with the fore and aft line of the hull always kept in a true line with its direction of travel. Turn the hull even the slightest to one side or the other and a ship underway will lose a fraction of speed. It is for this reason that ship owners go to the expense of installing automatic steering devices on their ships. It is not to make the helmsman's job easier, but to save fuel and money. They know each time the ship runs off course and must be brought back, the hull has turned slightly in the water and the speed has slowed. This causes extra fuel to be burned to get the ship to its destination. A constant turning of the hull, repeated over the length of the voyage, can be very expensive. Also in forcing the ship back on course the rudder must be turned to one side and then the other. This also will slow the ship. To prove a ship can be slowed by turning the rudder out to one side or the other, allow me to relate another piloting fact.

When I am about to leave the ship at the pilot station with the pilot launch drifting to starboard several ship lengths away, I have the ship running at half speed ahead (perhaps eight or nine knots) depending on the ship. When abeam of the launch, I order the rudder hard right, and place the engine on Dead Slow Ahead. The ship begins to swing around, and by the time it is at right angles to the original course, the launch is alongside the ship and throttling along with the ship at four to five knots. This rapid turning of the ship produces a large reduction in speed in a short time.

Because of the transfer factor, it is clear why the pilot of a ship will hold course when surrounded by numerous smaller vessels. He is reluctant to place nearby vessels operating in the transfer area into danger because a boat ahead will not make room for the ship. My motto is: let the captain causing the tight situation eat the problem he causes.

When in front of a ship underway, be fair to the other vessels around you. Do not remain too long in front of a ship, forcing the ship to turn and miss you. This places other nearby vessels in jeopardy who are hanging helplessly off to the side of the ship right in the middle of the transfer area!

The danger to any smaller vessel off to the side of a ship going into a sharp turn is great. In many respects the ship is out of control, even though it is slowing all the time. **When near a ship, and other vessels are fooling around ahead of the ship causing problems, be alert for that sudden course change and know the ship very possibly is going to come at you on the swing. You may find yourself in the transfer area!**

Again, observing the diagram closely, it is clear that when the rudder aboard a ship is placed hard right or hard left, the bow will first swing a few degrees to the opposite side—just enough to nail a private boat unfortunate enough to wind up under the bow of a ship. The reason this swing takes place, I have been told, is because of the sudden shifting of water pressure against each side of the rudder. I see it happen every time I order a course change at half or full speed. I am not even sure that a great number of shipmasters are aware of it. **If for some reason you happen to find yourself close under the bow of some ship, it might be a good thing to know so you can anticipate a problem.**

Another thing to bear in mind: **just because a ship is steaming down the bay with a bone in her teeth, does not mean it will not suddenly and without warning change course!** Just don't be nearby when it happens. You could easily be run over and wind up on the evening news as an item!

Chapter Twelve

Currents

At some time in your boating career I know you have been caught in a swirling tide rip and quickly found yourself headed back in the direction from which you came. Later you may have watched a ship steam past and just knew something as large as that could not be affected by the current. Right? Wrong!

Ships are affected by currents, even the biggest vessel afloat. They may not turn around one hundred and eighty degrees, but they can and are turned to one side or the other by a force of moving water pushing against the ship. Some currents, if from ahead, slow the vessel's speed over the ground. Or if from astern, they hurry the ship along to its destination. It can push a ship sideways if coming from any quarter with strength. Right here is a good time to tell you how a combination of a ship and strong currents can get you into trouble.

As you know by now, it is the wheel wash running past the rudder that gives the ship the ability to guide itself along an intended track or course. The weaker the water force the more sluggish the ship will answer the helm, and the longer time required to change the ship's heading. To illustrate my point allow me to tell you another Panama Canal story about the dangers of a ship losing control and coming to harm because the pilot lost to a strong propeller wash hitting against the rudder.

A friend of mine was departing the seaward lock chamber at Miraflores Locks on the Pacific side with a deeply loaded ship. At the moment he gave the order to cast off the locomotive wires holding the ship in the middle of the lock chamber the ship was making a speed of three knots, the top speed of the locomotives in the towing mode. The hold over water in the lock chamber was rolling out at three or four knots along with the ship. This meant the rudder was sitting in dead water and could not be used to steer the ship. The pilot, as he had done thousands of times before, ordered Dead Slow Ahead on the engine in order to steer the ship out of the locks. To his horror the engine failed to turn over when the air was shot to it. The immediate and negative results: the ship quickly went ashore on the nearby bank less than two hundred feet away. Because the propeller was not turning to provide the necessary wheel wash against the rudder. The type of current I have just mentioned running with the ship out of the lock chamber is a **following current.**

1—**Following currents** — A following current pushing at the stern of a ship can be one of the most dangerous and unhandy. The following current is one that pushes the ship along at a faster rate of speed than her engine produces in still water. Just as long as the ship keeps sufficient power on the engine to produce a strong flow of water past the rudder, the vessel can be steered straight and true with little problem. However, with following current, the more a ship reduces speed on the engine thus reducing the flow of water past the rudder, the less control the pilot has at his command to keep the ship on course. If the current is running swift and the pilot is forced to reduce speed, the ship has a great tendency to broach from side to side. And worse, if the engine is stopped completely, the ship's steering will become sluggish and very likely useless as experienced by my friend leaving the Miraflores Lock Chamber. **Be aware that if you are close to a ship in a following current and you force the ship to suddenly slow down, you may be in some danger due to lack of steering control aboard the ship.**

Following currents in a channel where the ship's maneuvering room is restricted because of size, depth and channel width, is fraught with great danger to a small nearby vessel. In my career I have over-taken many small vessels who retained their right of way down the center of the channel no matter how many danger blasts I let go on the whistle. Think on this if you will. When the pilot aboard the ship cannot slow the engine to run any speed below eight or nine knots, and the current is pushing the ship along at another three or four knots, a small boat that will not give way is courting disaster because there is very little the pilot can do to avoid another vessel when it comes too close. **It would be advisable if you are in an area of swift currents, and a ship is bearing down on your position, pull over far enough—soon enough—so the pilot will know early which side to pass with a fair margin of safety!**

2—**Lateral currents** — A lateral current is one striking the ship from one side or the other. This current in certain locations can and will shove a ship off its intended course track to a considerable degree unless corrective action is taken early. The only way a pilot can overcome this setting action is to steer a heading at an angle to the course. This angle is called **leeway.** Every pilot, as a result of not applying enough leeway in a lateral current, has found his ship much closer to a point of land, shoal, buoy or other vessel than was safe. Some pilots have gone aground or struck a rock because they failed to apply enough leeway in a strong current or high wind.

When out in your craft and you know or suddenly find that a strong current is setting you across the channel, be aware the ship you meet may be heading into the current and will appear headed in one direction while actually traveling in a different direction. Many times I have seen the captain of a smaller boat surprised when my ship moved down toward his position while seeming to head off in a different direction. Remember, in an area with a strong lateral current: **the ship you see in the distance may be steering or headed in one direction while actually setting down laterally on your position at a rapid and fearsome rate. It could be dangerous to your health!**

Chapter Thirteen

Winds

There are many occasions when the wind will affect the sideways or lateral movement of a ship to a far greater degree than the current ever will. I am sure you have experienced the same thing with your own vessel. It is obvious why this is so. A far greater portion of many vessels sit above the surface of the water rather than below it, thus giving the wind a large area to blow against. In the piloting trade this is called the "**Sail Area.**"

For instance, when piloting in a strong current, a pilot may set a ship's course four or five degrees to the right or left to off-set the force of a current pushing against the side of the ship. With a strong wind blasting against the ship the course may be set forty or fifty degrees off the basic course track. This is called "**Leeway.**" When applying leeway to the compass course, the vessel will be heading in one direction, **while actually traveling over the ground in a different direction. It is the ship traveling in a different direction other than it appears to be that you must recognize and deal with!**

The recommendation I make is: **If the wind is blowing strong watch the approaching ship and try to determine the actual direction of travel. And second, give the ship room to fight the wind rather than crowd his course and position. The ship may need more sea room due to circumstances unknown or not obvious to you.** In some strong winds I have steered as much as fifty and sixty degrees off the planned course.

Chapter Fourteen

The Vessel Traffic System

VTS—The letters stand for the words "**Vessel Traffic System.**" These words are becoming more and more important on our nation's waterways. In recent years they have brought about a change for the pilot that has made his work much easier and to a large degree safer for all the users of our inland seas. Unless you are the captain of a commercial vessel you are probably unaware of this system. If you do know about it I am pleased. The VTS in the United States is administered and operated by the United States Coast Guard and they do an excellent job. They deserve and should be given a great deal more credit than presently acknowledged for doing a very difficult, and at times trying job, and doing it with a sense of pride, dedication and professionalism.

The Federal Rules for the VTS are published and described in the code of Federal Regulations, Sub Chapter P, Title 33.

Contact the nearest United States Coast Guard office for information concerning the VTS in your area.

The purpose of the VTS is to prevent collisions and groundings, and to protect the navigable waters from environmental harm. It is not my purpose in this book to write down all the information available to the public contained in a pamphlet produced by the United States Coast Guard entitled, "**Vessel Traffic Service Operating Manual,**" but rather to point out the more pertinent facts relating to this publication as it directly relates to the ship and a private boat. I recommend you get a copy of this small manual and study it.

The VTS in its construction and make up is a network of traffic lanes (Inbound & Outbound), called TSS, "**Traffic**

Separation System." The TSS, is 1,000 yards wide, divided by a Separation Lane 500 yards wide, and marked by large sea buoys at the turning junctions. It is, in effect, a path back and forth to the ocean, and between ports. Vessels operating within the VTS area are monitored by the United States Coast Guard **"Vessel Traffic Center"** using late model radar sets. In conjunction with the radar sets the Vessel Traffic Center receives and broadcasts information necessary and helpful to the mariner by VHF radio. However the Coast Guard cautions they may not have the latest information or up to the minute knowledge of all hazardous circumstances.

It may interest you to know that in the past, your vessel's position may have been called to the attention of a pilot aboard some ship after the VTC observed you on the radar set near or in the Traffic Lanes, and it appeared you might get into trouble.

Under normal circumstances, the United States Coast Guard does not exercise direct control over vessels in the VTS area. They caution that the captain and pilot of every vessel is responsible for the safe and prudent navigation of his vessel. The VTC can and does, from time to time, exert control over vessel movements during conditions of vessel congestion, weather, and reduced visibility or other hazardous conditions. Additionally the master or pilot of a vessel in the VTS area must comply with such direction in a timely manner.

All commercial vessels must participate in the VTS, and must have on board a working VHF radio set monitoring specified channels.

A note of interest: small commercial vessels and tugs with tows many times choose (and are allowed by the VTC) to proceed outside the Traffic Lanes. This leaves the Lanes clear for the much bigger and faster ships. Action by these commercial vessels traveling outside the lanes just might be a hint for you when thinking about your own safety.

Ships follow the path of the traffic lanes day and night while underway in the VTS area. Fortunately the traffic lanes are well defined on the charts. See page 53.

Small boats under the VTS regulations should not impede the passage of ships operating in the traffic lanes. The captain

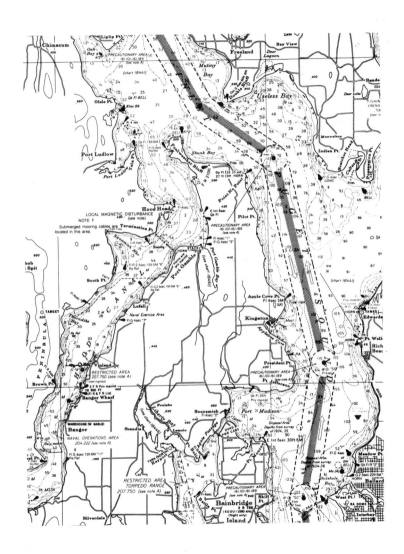

53

of a small boat sailing in the VTS area should observe all the regulations when entering, leaving or crossing the traffic lanes. Use the method recommended by the Coast Guard in the pamphlet.

Entering or leaving the traffic lanes—do so with as little an angle as possible. In other words, ease into and out of the Lanes.

Crossing the Traffic Lanes—do so at a direct angle to the flow of traffic. This means get across as quickly as you can.

Anchoring in the Traffic Lanes—do not drop the hook in the Traffic Lanes. In other words, keep the lanes free and clear so the ships will not have to turn out of the lane to get around you.

As a pilot, I would add this: don't stop and drift in the middle of the traffic lane, even if the fish are biting. The fish you catch might weigh many tons and have a propeller on the end and a bulbous bow on the other.

The regulations point out that large ships and tugs with tows are limited in just what they can do when it comes to stopping and turning quickly to avoid running you down.

Two of the most important points covered concerning the ships you meet in the traffic lanes are: number one: the ships and other commercial vessels are navigating up and down well defined traffic lanes, all clearly marked on the charts, and monitored by the United States Coast Guard for your protection and guidance. Number two: all ships have on board several VHF radios tuned to at least two channels and somtimes more.

What does the foregoing mean to the captain of a private boat? Very little I am afraid. But to the readers of this book it will mean a great deal. It will help eliminate many of the misunderstandings that happen between ships and small boats concerning just what are the intentions of the other, even in thick fog.

The traffic lanes themselves, in the case of my pilotage district, are 1.2 miles wide and take up very little room when compared to the total water area of the region. One of the favorable items about these lanes is that private boats are not restricted at any time from entering or using the lanes. The lanes are merely a path charted for commercial vessels to travel so they will not endanger the public good. They are clearly marked so the smaller vessels know with certainty just where these large ships will be traveling in their hurried way back and forth between the ocean and the inland ports. Actually the positioning of the lanes and junction buoys do hinder to some degree the quick passage of a sea-going vessel because the ship must steam extra miles to conform to the lanes as laid out by the Coast Guard. It's a small price to pay to protect the general public and other craft. Pilots and shipmasters welcome the traffic lanes as a boon to safe passage of their vessels during fair weather and foul. Today with the traffic lanes in place and working, every commercial vessel knows the other is in the proper lane and on his side of the channel. Quite a pleasant change from the days when everyone was steaming his own separate way without radio contact.

In the years before traffic lanes and radios, even with radar, ships and tugboats suffered many collisions because these vessels could and did steer in any direction. They were often on a side of the channel claimed by another vessel. Today, fortunately, the United States Coast Guard quickly calls to task, over the VHF radio, a vessel for departing into another vessel's area.

1—Changing course around the VTS area — One of the first things to recognize about the ship you see in the distance is the fact he is steaming toward you down a traffic lane that is well known to him and should be to you. The lane is clearly marked on the chart for the area.

Second, you may feel fairly certain the pilot will remain on track, on course, and running at top speed in this traffic lane until he reaches the next buoy at a turning juncture. You can bet in most cases the pilot will not alter his course even once if the path ahead is clear and remains so until he is past your position.

Third, when a pilot is faced with the fact a small boat has entered the traffic lanes and is moving toward the ship on a collision bearing and will not haul over, the ship will at some point be forced to haul course and perhaps go outside the Lanes. This jeopardizes the safety of nearby boats that keep clear of the ship in the Lane until the charging chunk of metal has passed.

It only makes good sense to learn where the traffic lanes are and their direction of travel, along with the location and color of the huge junction/turning buoys!

In the traffic lanes, you as a private boat commander, have a distinct advantage in keeping out of danger compared to the pilot aboard a ship. You are aware from observation the approximate course the pilot will maintain while the ship is in the traffic lane. You also know the pilot will only change course as necessary to avoid other vessels. When meeting private boats the pilot enjoys none of these advantages. The destination of each private boat the pilot observes running back and forth before the ship is unknown to him. To further complicate it for the pilot, many of the private boats will travel in one direction for a time, then change course for no apparent reason. Unfortunately this course change is often done directly in front of the ship and so close it causes real concern aboard the ship.

If you sometimes wonder why a ship will wait until you are close aboard before changing course, there is a simple explanation. Years ago I used to change course early and at a good distance in an attempt to encourage a smaller vessel to do likewise, thus clearing up any passing confusion. Very often the early course change is a mistake because the private boat may change course back and forth several times before you reach him, forcing the ship to change back and forth like a drunk driving an automobile down the road.

If you meet a ship and he changes course away from you, why not do the same so it is obvious you also plan to keep clear! Beware!!! If you blow a whistle signal it cannot be heard aboard today's modern ships!

The point of all this is: you as captain of a private boat know your plan of action, the pilot does not. You as commander of your own vessel can quickly figure out the course and direction of travel of an approaching ship, and be fairly certain the course will not change (except at turning junctions), or as a last resort where the pilot is forced to take evasive action against some nearby small vessel. *Always the pilot has no idea what action a small boat will take as it approaches.* **The private boat can, and very often will, *change course and speed quickly around ships.*** This the ship *cannot* do.

In many cases during a meeting or crossing situation it lies with you and you alone, the small boat commander, to save your own life. Because the ship cannot maneuver fast enough to keep clear, the burden to keep clear frequently falls heavily on the shoulders of the small boat captain. It's one hell of a responsibility!

2. Radio communications around the VTS area — believe it or not, you as the captain of a non-commercial vessel, can talk with the pilot aboard any ship you see! All ships underway have at least two and sometimes three VHF radio channels open on a bridge listening for calls addressed to his ship.

One channel is used to talk with and listen to the Coast Guard Vessel Traffic Center regarding important information about the movement of other vessels, hazardous conditions, developing situations ahead of the ship, and any additional information useful that will enable the ship to arrive at its destination in a safe and timely manner. Also information about large concentrations of pleasure boats and private fishing boats is broadcast to ships as general information. In my pilotage area the VTS channel is 14.

A second channel used is number (13). This channel is known as the (Bridge to Bridge) channel. It is used by pilots, watch officers on ferry boats, and tugboat captains and mates, to exchange information. Most important it is used to make passing arrangements when there is some doubt about what another vessel might do. I well remember the wild days before ships carried radios on the bridge, and passing arrangements were made by guess and passing signals. The signals may or may not have been heard by the other vessel. The number and frequency of collisions that took place in those days gave testimony to what a crap shoot it was. Unfortunately not much has changed today betwen the pilot and the captain of a small vessel.

To avoid this reckless shooting craps with destiny, why not buy a radio and use it when near the path of a ship underway?

It may surprise you, but very few ships listen to channel (16) while steaming through the inland waters in areas where the Coast Guard has set up Vessel Traffic Systems. Instead they guard channels (13) and (14).

I do not, I repeat I do not know of any ships that listen to, or even have aboard, the very popular (CB) radio.

Ninety nine percent of the ships I go aboard have only one VHF radio set mounted on the bridge. Usually this radio can only monitor one channel at a time. I tune to Channel (14) so as to be in touch with the Traffic Center. At the time of coming aboard a ship, I carry with me an over-night bag containing, among other things, a hand held VHF radio. (Years ago these radios were called walkie-talkies.) I prop this hand set against the forward wheel house windows right after I tune it to channel (13). This allows me to send and receive calls from other vessels. (Also the Coast Guard has the capability to contact me on channel 13.) Later, upon approaching the dock, I switch channels and carry this hand set out to the wing of the bridge and talk to the tugboats assisting the ship during the berthing operation.

Some of my pilot friends have small boats of their own and spend considerable time out on the water away from Piloting.

Some of these men take their (piloting) VHF radios with them and mount them with channel (14) turned on. This way they have a radio at a cheap price, and very little trouble. May I suggest you consider such a set yourself. A used radio can be purchased at a reasonable cost, and will give you protection in case of an accident or emergency. If you had such a set you would be able to monitor the Coast Guard channel, and also call any ship you might have a problem with. However, limit conversations to necessary and pertinent business, such as meeting and passing arrangements. **I am not suggesting you call every ship you see. Only those ships nearby whom you think might like to know your intentions.**

But how do I call this ship, you might ask. Many times the name of the ship cannot be seen because the ship is too far away to see the letters painted on the bow. Because of this, calling in the blind is used many times a year by commercial vessels when they do not know the name of another vessel in the vicinity. Calling in the blind works as follows: Suppose your vessel is located two miles south of Dolphin Point. You are steering due north, with Dolphin Point lying some distance away over your starboard bow. Suddenly a ship appears around the north side of Dolphin Point, steering due west. Immediately you know the ship has the right of way and will hold his course and speed. Watching the ship, you learn the bearing is not changing. Both vessels are on a collision course. At this point you know something must be done by you to avoid an impact. The first action is yours because you are burdened and must give way, either by changing course or by slowing the speed of your vessel.

As the two vessels draw near, the pilot begins to worry about what your actions are going to be. Whether you are going to act at all, or hold on until you are so close he must act to keep from hitting you. Bear in mind what I said earlier about the distance fore-shortening to the pilot aboard the ship, and the distance fore-lengthening to smaller craft. However, you can call a ship in the blind by saying: "Calling the ship north of Dolphin Point steering west. This is the boat Blue Water standing by on channel thirteen."

The pilot will answer. "Blue Water, this is the Motor Vessel Sea Wolf. Go ahead."

"Sea Wolf, this is Blue Water. My position is approximately two miles south of Dolphin Point. Hold your course and speed. I will slow down and pass astern of you."

"Thank you, Blue Water. I will maintain course and speed. Good day."

It is best to keep your conversation to a bare minimum. Do not clutter the airways. Also the pilot may be busy with other duties requiring immediate attention.

Obviously one of the additional advantages in having a radio aboard your vessel would be for emergency situations. Accidents are bound to happen which can turn quickly into a happening beyond your control. You may well require outside help, and in a hurry. A VHF radio to summon help or to

59

inform others of your plight and assistance needed may save your life or that of someone you love. Allow me to illustrate for a moment.

Several years ago while underway one night, the traffic over the radio had been light. Aboard the ship things were quiet on the bridge except for the hum of the radars and the forced air blowers whispering in the background pushing fresh air into the wheelhouse. The helmsman was doing an excellent job at the wheel. Behind me the mate on watch was keeping silent watch on the radar as he regularly plotted the position across the chart. Perched in the high pilot's chair at the forward wheelhouse windows with six hundred feet of ship spread out before me, I looked out over a smooth sea completely devoid of a single craft.

Suddenly over the radio sounded the desperate voice of a man calling the Coast Guard asking for immediate medical assistance for his wife bleeding profusely from a gash in her neck. The wonderful men in the Coast Guard Vessel Traffic Center quickly gathered the necessary information, and calmed the poor fellow pleading for help. I timed it by the ship's clock, and in less than two minutes help was speeding on its way. I tell this story because it points up a very unusual circumstance. The vessel was not underway, but tied to a float at a small marina with a telephone some two blocks away. As a result of having a radio aboard, help was quickly provided to the captain's wife by shoreside people. There was a reassuring coordination between the vessel's radio, the United States Coast Guard and a medical team ashore. **The radio saved a human life, which was well worth the sum of money spent, don't you think?**

Other pilots and I not only use radios to send and receive messages but to monitor the radio traffic of other vessels. It is vital for a pilot while in charge of a fast moving ship to keep abreast of developing situations ahead of the ship. At times in the past this constant listening to what is happening miles ahead of my ship has saved me a great deal of trouble and aggravation. Who knows? If you get a radio you may have a lot of fun listening to and using the radio. There is a good chance the radio will make your trip both pleasant and much safer, not only for yourself but for other vessels around you.

Chapter Fifteen
Crowded Sea Lanes

It is often said among pilots that winter time is the best time of all to work at the profession of navigating ships through the inland waters of the United States. This is in spite of the winter winds and lousy weather. Why would a pilot say this when winter conditions make many of the jobs miserable, wet, cold and much more difficult to do properly especially in darkness and poor visibility?

Because it is the time of year when all the commercial and private fishing boats are laid up for the winter, and the private citizen has secured his boat in a safe moorage. It is the time of year when neither group will be out again in great numbers until spring. It is the time of the year when the ship does not have to compete with smaller vessels for the limited space in the shipping lanes. After reading the foregoing statement you are probably thinking: "That egotistical pilot must think the whole area belongs exclusively to him and the ship." Let me hasten to assure you this is not the case at all. Many of the pilots have boats of their own and understand the waters are the property of all the people and are to be used to the fullest without bias or restriction.

Then comes the good weather of spring and summer. Thousands of private boats take to the waterways in mass. Now begins a time of worry and stress for the pilot when he tries to make his way safely and in a timely manner through this rush of boats, all fleeing the stifling atmosphere of the city for the fresh sea breezes over the open water. The next months will be a game of dodging from one collision situation to another for the pilot. Each happening involves a vessel much smaller than the ship, and much handier to maneuver. The majority of these vessels will be coming at the ship from forward of the beam at speeds from dead in the water up to thirty knots. In the back of every pilot's mind lurks the hope and prayer that he will never be in charge of a ship that runs down a smaller vessel.

In my work on Puget Sound in the summer it is not unusual to round a prominent point of land and find myself looking down a channel filled with more boats than I have time to count. The first thing I usually do is cuss a lot. Next I try to find a path to pass through. When it looks impossible, it's about the time I begin to wish I were some place else.

Every pilot you meet while aboard your boat could easily keep out of your way and avoid a dangerous close quarters passing situation if he knew for certain what every small vessel ahead of his ship was planning to do. It is this uncertainty over what a small boat is going to do with his course and speed that makes the job of piloting in and around small boats a game of dodge and weave. As you can imagine, a ship is a very large creature to perform this exercise.

To avoid this crap shoot of: "I wonder what the other guy is going to do?" most pilots will attempt to set a course and hold to it when approaching one or more smaller craft. This for two reasons: one is to get to the destination as quickly as possible, but more important, to let the captain of a private boat know the direction the ship intends to steer while proceeding through the area. Unfortunately this attempt to set and maintain a course will continue to meet with failure time after time mainly because the commanders of private vessels are unaware of the pilot's intention. I find it almost impossible for a ship to keep and maintain one single course through a large number of vessels, or even a few boats for that matter. Not when every boat is headed in a different direction all at different speeds.

A thing to remember: **A ship in your area is trying desperately to pass through as quickly as possible. To do so, it will immediately set one course and, if at all possible, stick with it to the next turning point.** This positive and straight forward action is in great contrast to the courses and speeds set by private boats. Each is bound for a different spot, leaving the pilot with no clear indication of just where they are headed. **Over the years, time after time, I have seen thousands of small vessels change course when very close to my ship. A sure way to confuse any pilot!**

A pilot on the bridge of a ship, because of the higher elevation, use of radar, and information coming in by VHF radio, most probably is aware of hazards up ahead, or the need to take action to protect the ship and your boat long before the commander of a private boat learns what is taking place. **In a quickly changing situation, other pilots and I are just as concerned about a smaller boat's safety and the need to protect your well being, as you the captain are!**

This protective attitude is due in part to training during a previous sea-going career, and the tradition of the sea that says the strong shall protect the weak.

Chapter Sixteen

Diagrams

It is often said: "One picture is worth a thousand words." I hope this is true.

So as not to bore you with a book filled with information and instructions about The Rules of the Road that can better be learned elsewhere, I have made a few diagrams that will show you in a practical manner how to avoid a dangerous situation for yourself when doubt sets in around ships underway. At the same time it will give the pilot aboard the ship you meet a good indication of just what your course of action will be.

There are many variations to this basic set of diagrams. I am sure in the future you will know what to do around ships if you give just a little thought to what I have shown here, coupled with what I have just written.

Diagram 1. In this situation the ship at the bottom of the page and the boat ahead of the ship at the top of the page are steaming in a direct line, one behind the other, and both on the same course. The ship at twenty knots is rapidly overtaking the boat at ten knots.

The ship is hemmed in by the many surrounding boats, all of whom will pass clear according to the pilot's calculations. But if the ship finds it necessary to alter course to move around the boat at the top of the page, then the pilot is forced into a possible collision with the other boats spread out on either side.

I recommend the boat directly ahead of the ship alter his course to either the port or starboard to allow the ship behind to slip past. I recommend this even if the captain of the vessel ahead believes the overtaking ship will pass clear without his changing course. And most important, he would be wise to

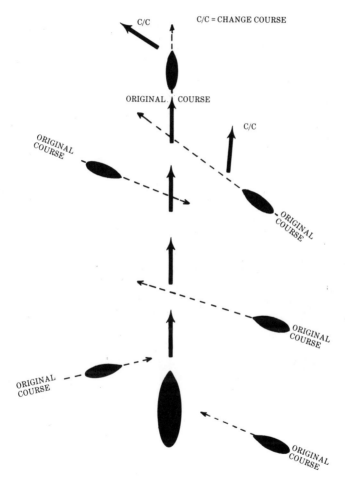

C/C = CHANGE COURSE

Diagram 1

alter course substantially to make it plain to the pilot he notes the ship moving up astern.

However, bear in mind it is useless to change course only a few degrees. It is impossible for the pilot to note a small change. Additionally, it would be prudent to change early because of the chance the people aboard the ship may not see a boat ahead in time to avoid running it down. At night do make a substantial course change and put that important extra wide margin of sea room between yourself and the fast moving ship astern.

Why hang on to your course with a ship bearing down on you just because the pilot has not blown an overtaking signal? You are in great danger when you remain in a ship's path. Why not be a courteous seaman and consider the safety of the other boats in your area? Give thought to the danger they will suddenly find themselves facing if the ship is forced to make a course change in their direction. **Or worse for you, the pilot may not see your vessel!**

Diagram 2. The current, as I mentioned earlier, can be a problem for something as large as a ship, especially in a restricted channel. The current can set the ship sideways a considerable distance and it would not be apparent to a smaller vessel. As a result, a ship can set down upon a boat in a short period of time.

At other times ships are so heavily loaded, with so much hull area under the water, the current will affect the ship to a much greater degree than it would a light draft ship. Often a deep draft ship cannot move very far out of the channel, if at all. To do so would cause the ship to go aground on nearby reefs or shoals. More than one ship has been forced ashore because another vessel crowded its course, and to avoid a collision the pilot chose the shore.

Please keep in mind, if at times you think the pilot is acting like a hog and wants more than his fair share of the channel, it may be the ship needs the deeper water which just happens to be in your exact spot at the time.

I recommend everyone alter course as shown by the arrows, and give the ships room to get around and pass safely. One thing I should point out in this diagram: the southbound ship

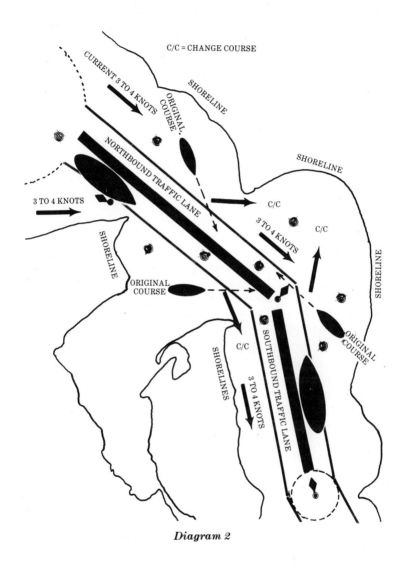

C/C = CHANGE COURSE

SHORELINE

CURRENT 3 TO 4 KNOTS

ORIGINAL COURSE

SHORELINE

NORTHBOUND TRAFFIC LANE

3 TO 4 KNOTS

C/C

3 TO 4 KNOTS

C/C

SHORELINE

SHORELINE

ORIGINAL COURSE

ORIGINAL COURSE

C/C

SHORELINES

3 TO 4 KNOTS

SOUTHBOUND TRAFFIC LANE

Diagram 2

is moving with the current on his stern and will be coming down on the boats at a speed much faster than the engine will produce. And if the pilot is forced to slow the engine he will have much less control over the steering of the vessel than if he were heading into the current.

In a swift flowing current as shown on the preceding page when two ships meet, the pilots face a rapidly changing situation requiring long range planning to safely pass clear of each other. Adding a number of smaller craft, all wishing to move out into the area ahead of the ships, is to create a situation that is not only dangerous for the smaller boats but the ships as well.

In the swift current, pilots will fight to maintain their track along the course line so as to maintain as much sea room away from the shore as possible.

It has been my experience, smaller vessels will bravely forge out into a traffic lane feeling confident one or more ships in the vicinity will keep clear of them. Too late they discover they have steered into a position between two swift ships hurtling down on them and are unable to clear by their action.

When finally these unfortunate souls realize they are about to become the live meat in a steel sandwich they panic and change course, first in one direction then the other. In an attempt to escape, they will often change course across the bow of a ship in close, giving the pilot the scare of his life as he maneuvers the ship to avoid wiping out the smaller vessel. Numerous times I have noticed that a small boat in this type of situation will change its course across my bow, not once or twice, but three or four times, leaving me to really sweat until finally we cleared, sometimes by only a few feet.

Diagram 3. Here, the ship is being towed stern first down a narrow channel by a tug using its towline. The ship's engines are stopped with the rudder amidship. The ship is fitted with a bow thruster which the pilot is using to push the bow from side to side. The pilot has his hands full maintaining the ship's position in the middle of the channel because a ship is not designed to travel stern first and will suddenly sheer one direction or the other in what I call a **Dive.** When a ship takes a dive, the ship will often move quickly to one side of the channel.

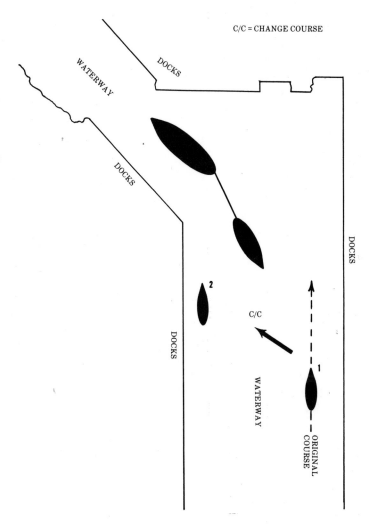

Diagram 3

69

In the diagram boat number "1" is in a bad position because the ship will be moving over to his side of the channel. The ship could very easily and quickly wind up in the corner area just ahead of boat "1." This is a very unsafe spot for a boat to find itself against a heavy, cumbersome ship.

Additionally, if the ship picks up too much speed moving astern, the pilot will be forced to kick the engine ahead to slow the ship's movement astern. This action is very dangerous for the boat. The powerful wash of the propeller can easily sink the boat, or perhaps wash the boat under the dock causing serious damage to the boat and inflicting injury on those aboard.

If boat number "2" holds his position and side of the channel the ship will most likely pass without incident.

Diagram 4. Here, a ship is bound to the entrance of a channel. The problem for the pilot of the inbound ship is not the two vessels at anchor, but the private boat in close to the docks.

By its position behind the anchored container ship, the boat is effectually hidden from view to the inbound pilot. It is obvious the boat underway is headed directly into the path of the inbound ship.

It will come as quite a shock to the pilot when suddenly a boat comes around the stern of the container ship. It may surprise the pilot, but it could turn out to be a most dangerous situation for the boat to find itself close to and directly in the path of a ship that is greatly restricted as to just what can be done to miss hitting the boat.

It would be smart for the boat captain, when moving around ships at anchor in a crowded harbor, to keep a sharp lookout and, just as important, be prepared to maneuver quickly and take evasive action.

Diagram 5. In this case a ship is headed in to a dock. The pilot has carefully positioned the ship for the final approach. The ship is moving ahead in a straight line at a reduced speed. So as not to cause damage to the dock, the ship at this stage of its voyage must be kept carefully under control. This means the ship's head must not be turned or the ship allowed to set to either side.

70

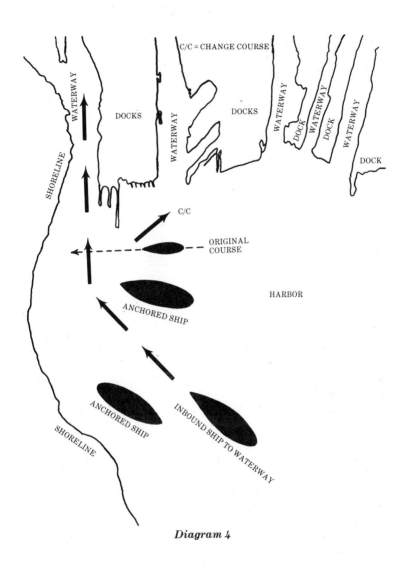

C/C = CHANGE COURSE

WATERWAY

DOCKS

WATERWAY

DOCKS

WATERWAY

WATERWAY

DOCK

WATERWAY

DOCK

WATERWAY

DOCK

SHORELINE

C/C

ORIGINAL
COURSE

HARBOR

ANCHORED SHIP

ANCHORED SHIP

INBOUND SHIP TO WATERWAY

SHORELINE

Diagram 4

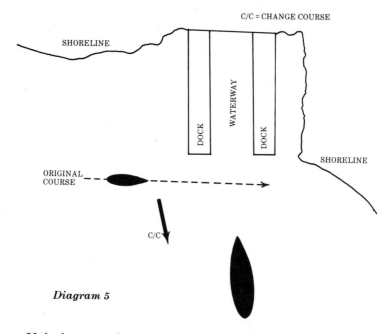

Diagram 5

If the boat continues across in front of the ship, and the pilot feels threatened because he suspects the boat cannot make it without risk of collision, he may start backing the engine. Unfortunately once he starts the engine going astern the ship will begin to twist sideways and turn her head away from the dock. Many a ship has struck the pier because the engine was backing at the time, and the pilot could not control the ship's head. **Many pilots feel a ship is out of control anytime the engine is going astern at a high number of revolutions.**

The boat should pass astern of the ship even if the boat captain believes with all his heart he has enough room to clear the ship. Think back to what was said earlier concerning the conflict between a small vessel and a ship about how far apart each believe they are from the other when approaching.

Not known to the majority of people out on the water is the fact that a ship's engine does not always back when tried. In this case, the boat could wind up shoved under the dock by a ship unable to stop because the engine could not be put into reverse.

72

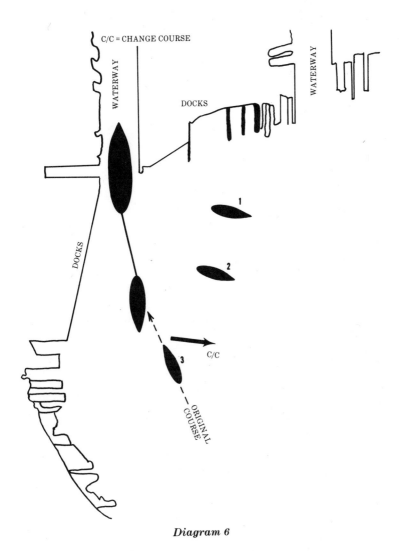

C/C = CHANGE COURSE

WATERWAY

DOCKS

WATERWAY

DOCKS

1

2

3

C/C

ORIGINAL COURSE

Diagram 6

73

Diagram 6. Again, a ship is being towed stern first out of a narrow channel into an open harbor. Because the ship has to be turned around after it clears the channel so as to proceed out of the harbor, boats number "1" and "2" are doing the safe thing. They are leaving the immediate area and giving the pilot room to swing the ship around.

But boat number "3" is proceeding into the area of the greatest danger and causing not only the pilot of the ship but the tugboat captain a great deal of concern.

I say the tugboat captain because a tugboat towing a ship on the tow line is always in a dangerous position. Not known to the boating public is the fact numerous tugboats over the years have been tipped onto their side and sunk with a loss of life while made fast to ships underway.

A tugboat can easily go into **"irons."** This means a tugboat on a tow line with a ship astern slips off to the side of the ship's direction of travel, and in so doing is restricted from maneuvering by the strain on the tow-line. The ship then quickly over-takes and by-passes the tugboat. This pulls the tug over onto its side (much like someone grabbing your arm and jerking you off balance causing you to fall down). But in this case the results are: one sunk tugboat and maybe death for all or part of the crew.

The captain of the private boat nearing the tug and ship should keep well clear because the captain of the tugboat has his hands full just trying to stay ahead of the moving ship towering over the stern of his tugboat.

In the situation shown, the tugboat captain can only avoid you by **placing his vessel in grave danger!**

Diagram 7. In this diagram we see a heavily loaded ship approaching an anchorage in preparation to dropping the hook. You note the anchorage is already filled with three anchored vessels. The space remaining for the inbound ship is severely limited.

The private boat drifting ahead of the ship should move out of the anchorage well ahead of time to let the pilot know he can come in without worrying about the area being cleared by the time the ship arrives at the spot to let the anchor go.

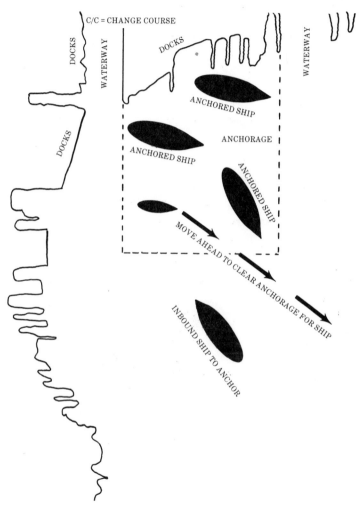

C/C = CHANGE COURSE

DOCKS

WATERWAY

DOCKS

DOCKS

WATERWAY

ANCHORED SHIP

ANCHORED SHIP

ANCHORAGE

ANCHORED SHIP

MOVE AHEAD TO CLEAR ANCHORAGE FOR SHIP

INBOUND SHIP TO ANCHOR

Diagram 7

75

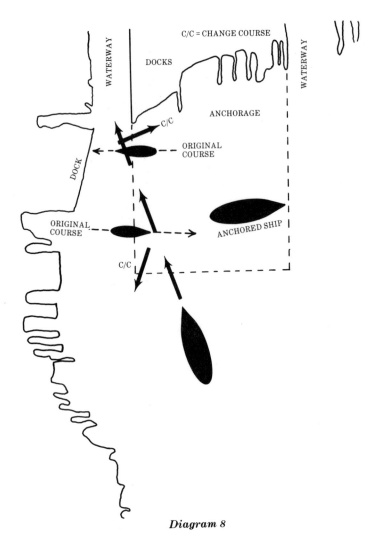

WATERWAY

C/C = CHANGE COURSE

DOCKS

WATERWAY

ANCHORAGE

C/C

DOCK

ORIGINAL
COURSE

ORIGINAL
COURSE

ANCHORED SHIP

C/C

Diagram 8

If you are wondering why the ship does not anchor in a different area, harbor regulations in most cases designate the anchorage area for ships. In other harbors, the exact spot for anchoring a ship is assigned by harbor authorities.

Diagram 8. It is clear the ship is headed directly toward a narrow channel entrance already blocked by two boats. The ship obviously must proceed into the channel before it can dock at its assigned berth. Very probably the fishing is good at this channel entrance and the boats are drifting with fishing lines in the water.

If the boats would move out of the way a short distance in a timely manner it would relieve the situation. The ship will be past in a very short time and the boats can quickly move back to their original positions.

You can count on one thing. The ship will and must get into the channel regardless of how reluctant the boats are to move. Why not move a little early? Keep in mind what was said earlier about the conflict over distances between ship and boats!

Diagram 9. Here the ship at the bottom of the page is holding its course and speed. The pilot is aware that all of the boats ahead will clear the ship because the bearings have all changed rapidly.

However boat number (2) is on a collision bearing. And if things don't change there will be a nasty situation.

Boat number (2) should change course early, and very substantially to let the pilot know he recognizes the situation and will relieve it. If boat number (2) does not do so the pilot will be forced to change the ship's course with the good possibility the other boats, who earlier were going to pass clear, will now be in a collision situation. This is certainly grossly unfair to all concerned.

Boat number (2) should change the course early in this case, and to the left. By this action the boat and ship will meet and pass down the side of each other in a very short time. As a bonus, at night the pilot will be able to keep a close watch on the boat's running lights for any sudden change.

Diagram 10. In this classical situation the ship really has no place to go. The ship can only hold course and speed due to

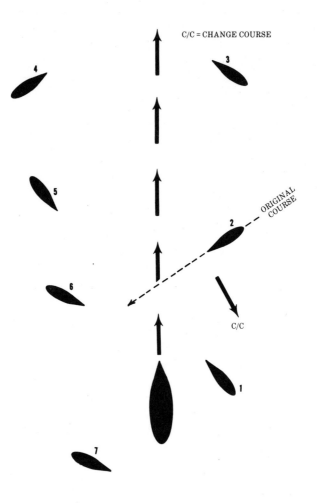

Diagram 9

78

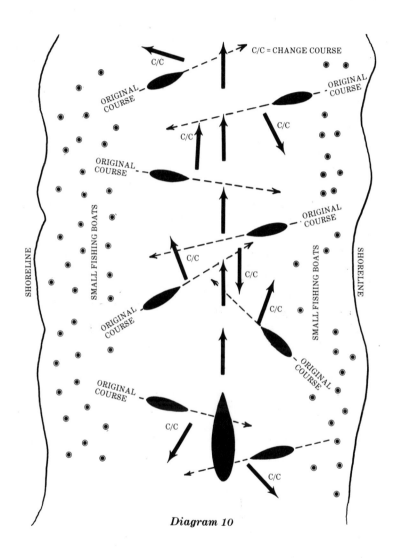

Diagram 10

the close proximity to the shore and the drifting sports fishing boats spread out on either side.

The prudent action would be for each boat to alter their heading substantially to let the pilot know they are going to keep clear because of the tight situation. This action will avoid what could be a potential disaster for everyone concerned if the ship has to start maneuvering around any number of private boats.

One thing you can count on, the ship will not in any case move his course track very much to either side if forced to alter course. Under no circumstances will the ship run too close to drifting fishing boats.

If the pilot is put in a box, and forced to twist and turn the ship to find a clear path ahead, he is going to do it right down through the middle of the private boats.

Please do not think I or any other pilot believes they should automatically have a path cleared ahead of the ship, and at all times be given the Right of Way.

What I do say: **If you can change course to ease a crossing situation with a ship, do so. You will make it safe for the boats around you. It makes little sense to hold on with a ship, refusing to give up the path ahead, when doing so jeopardizes some poor soul nearby!**

Diagram 11. Here we have two deeply loaded ships, the southbound ship a loaded tanker, and northbound a heavy bulk carrier.

It is obvious the tanker will sail free unless the pilot aboard the bulk carrier decides to change course hard to the left to escape the sailing vessel coming across his bow on a collision course. It is unlikely he would do so. But just suppose the pilot on the bulk carrier changes course a few degrees to go astern of the sailing vessel and the rudder jammed to the left. Then the real possibilities of a collision appear. If a collision should happen before the two ships could stop (and it is doubtful if they would be able to do so), there would be one heck of an explosion followed by the death of a number of crewmen aboard both ships.

The pilot aboard the bulk carrier, because of his deep draft, will attempt almost anything to keep from changing course to

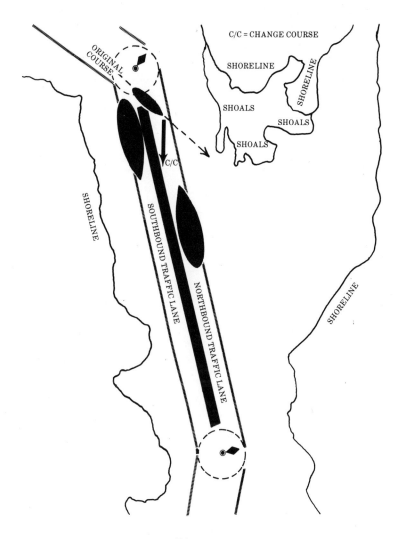

C/C = CHANGE COURSE

SHORELINE

SHOALS

SHOALS

SHOALS

ORIGINAL COURSE

C/C

SOUTHBOUND TRAFFIC LANE

NORTHBOUND TRAFFIC LANE

SHORELINE

SHORELINE

SHORELINE

Diagram 11

81

the right because of the shallow water in the shoal area.

The boat could greatly ease the situation by altering course so as to parallel the path of the two ships. Again, at the speed ships travel today, it would only be a short time until the two ships are past and gone.

Diagram 12. In this diagram all vessels are driving into a restricted area with little room for maneuvering. It is obvious the two ships, given their size, weight and speed, have little or no options to change course and keep clear of the smaller vessels mainly because of the close proximity of the shore.

It would completely clear the situation if the two boats would change course early and parallel the course track of their two respective overtaking ships.

At the speeds ships travel today it will not take long for the ships to pass. In addition the two boats would lose very little time by changing course a few degrees because the difference in running distance is so small it can be discounted.

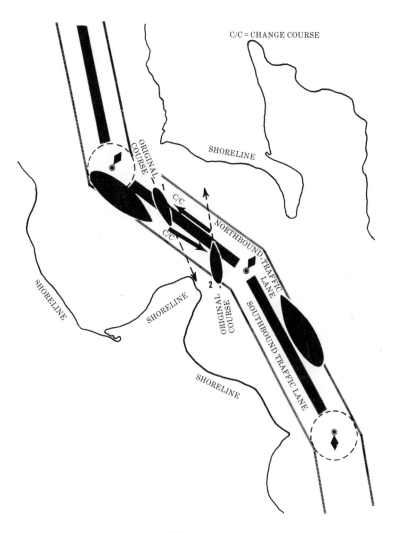

C/C = CHANGE COURSE

SHORELINE

ORIGINAL COURSE

C/C

C/C

NORTHBOUND TRAFFIC LANE

ORIGINAL COURSE

2

SHORELINE

SHORELINE

SHORELINE

SOUTHBOUND TRAFFIC LANE

Diagram 12

83

Chapter Seventeen
My Last Advice

Here at the end of my little tale I suppose I should say something profound, a word or two you can carry with you as we part. As I was putting these words down on page after page of paper I thought long and hard about just what that might be. Unhappily, I was unable to think up, let alone pass on, some great pronouncement of wisdom that would ring down through the ages. There are pilots I am sure who could and would be able to make a statement or two that would almost have seemed to have come down from a mountain etched in stone.

Years ago I sailed third officer under a captain whom I looked upon with love in my heart as a son might for an understanding father. I greatly respected this captain because of his winning ways with a ship. All the time I was with him, I never knew him to make a bad decision on the bridge. I remember one morning coming out of Yokohama, Japan, surrounded on all sides by ships with numerous small craft cutting across the traffic lanes. The captain kept the ship at full speed and blew the whistle so often and long the fireman in the engine room had to increase the fires in the boilers to keep up the steam pressure.

After an hour of this the captain turned to me with a twinkle in his eye and asked, "Do you know what all this whistling means to those boats out there, John, my boy?" He waved his arm toward the bow of the ship.

I answered, "No. I don't know."

He laughed and said just before he pulled on the whistle cord for another ear shattering blast, "That means get the hell out of the way. I'm coming through."

This, then, is my final word of wisdom to you: always act as if every ship you meet is commanded by my captain who is coming through and thereby save your life and those aboard who trust you.

One request: **Next time you pass, wave a greeting. If I see you, I will certainly wave back!**

A Short History of Pilotage

From the earliest writings of history, captains of vessels ranging in size from the smallest sailing ship to the atomic powered vessels of this modern day, have always employed pilots with local knowledge to guide their ships from the sea into a safe berth or anchorage.

Governments going back hundreds of years have instructed the pilot to conduct vessels under their charge in a timely and efficient manner without bringing harm to their own vessel, other vessels, other persons and possessions. This charge to the pilot, in some cases, is given under pain of death if the pilot should fail to perform successfully.

The Admiralty courts of England hundreds of years ago adopted the twelfth century law from the island of Orion off the coast of France, which said in Article XXII:

"If a pilot undertakes the conduct of a vessel, to bring her to St. Malo, or any other port, and fail therein, so as the vessel miscarry by reason of his ignorance in what he undertook, and the merchants sustain damage thereby, he shall be obliged to make full satisfaction for the same, if he hath wherewithal; and if not lose his head."

And Article XXIV of the same law provides:

"And if the master, or any one of his mariners, or any one of the merchants, cut off his head, they shall not be bound to answer for it; but before they do it, they must be sure he had not wherewith to make satisfaction."

Maritime law in the fourteenth century during the Roman empire noted a pilot's penalty as follows:

"He who cannot pay with his purse must suffer in his person."

In biblical times reading in the 27th chapter of Ezekiel pilots are talked about:

"Thy wise men, O Tyrus that were in thee, were they pilots."
"They riches, and they fairs, they mariners, and they pilots.
"The suburbs shall shake at the sound of thy pilots."
"And all that handle the oar, the mariners, and all the pilots of the sea,
shall come down from their ships."

We know that famous explorers of the past, such men as Columbus, Sebastian Cabot, Sir Francis Drake fighting the Spanish Armada, and Marco Polo, all used the services of pilots.

Perhaps most interesting of all is the fact "Amerigo Vespucci, for whom our country is named, carried the title "Chief Pilot" for the Spanish government in the year 1508.

Leading to more modern times it is generally agreed the present day pilots structure began in Holland perhaps as early as the mid 1700s, leading to pilotage acts all over the world structured much like my own pilotage district here in Washington state, whose act reads in part:

"The legislature finds and declares that it is the policy of the state of Washington to prevent the loss of human lives, loss of property and vessels, and to protect the marine environment through the sound application of compulsory pilotage provisions in certain state waters.

"The legislature further finds and declares that it is a policy of the state to have pilots experienced in the handling of vessels aboard vessels in certain of the state waters with prescribed qualifications and licenses issued by the state.

"It is the intent of the legislature to ensure against the loss of lives, loss or damage to property and vessels, and to protect the marine environment through the establishment of a board of pilotage commissioners representing the interests of the people of the state of Washington.

"It is the further intent of the legislature not to place in jeopardy Washington's position as an able competitor for waterborne commerce from other ports and nations of the world, but rather to continue to develop and encourage such commerce.

"No person shall pilot any vessel on waters covered unless such person be appointed and licensed to pilot such vessels on said waters.

"All pilots and applicants shall be subject to an annual physical examination by a physician chosen by the board.

"A pilot shall refuse a pilotage assignment if said pilot is physically or mentally fatigued or if said pilot has a reasonable belief that the assignment cannot be carried out in a competent and safe manner.

87

"The board shall have power on its own motion or, in its discretion, upon the written request of any interested party, to investigate the performance of pilotage services subject to this chapter and to suspend, withhold or revoke the license of any pilot for misconduct, incompetency, inattention to duty, intoxication or failure to perform his duties, or violation of any of the rules or regulations provided by the board for the government of pilots."

LATE NEWS RELEASE
SEATTLE TIMES
August 5, 1982

Tug hits stalled boat in Sound:
4 anglers escape serious injury

by Marjorie Jones
Times staff reporter

A Minnesota visitor suffered broken ribs and three other persons suffered minor hypothermia when their 25-foot pleasure craft was hit by a tug last night about four miles northwest of Shilshole Bay.

Walter Johnson, 62, Little Falls, Minn., suffered three broken ribs when he was pushed into the boat's transom. He was taken to Overlake Hospital in Bellevue, where he was treated and released.

Leslie N. Cole, 33, Bellevue, owner of the boat, and his two nephews, Christopher Aanes, 15, and Jason Aanes, 12, both of Fergus Falls, Minn., were in the water about 25 minutes before they were rescued by the tug. None required hospital treatment.

Cole said his boat went dead in the water after the four were fishing for salmon in Agate Bay. The accident took place about 10:30 p.m.

"We saw the tug a way off bearing down on us and tried frantically to get the engine started, but couldn't," Cole said. "I flashed the flashlight, but the lights kept coming.

"When the tug was about five feet away, I told my nephews to jump and they did. Then I told my father-in-law to jump, but he stayed on board."

The tug, the Edith Lovejoy, owned by Puget Sound Freight Lines, struck the pleasure craft portside near the stern, Cole said. Hugh Marsh, marine operations manager for the freight lines, said an investigation is under way and there would be no comment until all the facts are known.

Cole and his nephews were caught in the tug's wake. Christopher had a life preserver and began to swim the 25 feet back to the boat. He made it, but Cole and Jason were sharing one preserver and had difficulty swimming against the wake, Cole said.

"Then we looked up and the barge was coming by, and we started to swim frantically back so we wouldn't get run over by it," Cole said.

Apparently the tug crew realized it had struck something and began to turn around.

The tug crew threw them a lifeline and life ring. By then, Cole's preserver had been washed away.

Cole and his nephew were taken aboard and the pleasure craft was tied to the tug. A Coast Guard cutter arrived about 11:30 p.m. and took them to Shilshole for treatment by paramedics.

Weary and sore today, Cole described the experience as an "ordeal, an extremely close call."

"We're extremely fortunate to be alive," Cole said. "We were lucky the boat, which had a full gas tank, did not explode, and I don't think we could have lasted another 10 minutes in the water. Our legs were numb when they pulled us from the water."

Cole said the pleasure craft is his ninth boat. It did not appear to have received structural damage and was moored at Shilshole this morning.

As for the accident, Cole called it a "freak thing."

"They just didn't see us," he said.

To add insult to injury, the four didn't catch any salmon, but took home some cod.

—Reprinted by permission of *The Seattle Times*, copyright 1982.

90